DEAR WORLD

This Large Print Book carries the
Seal of Approval of N.A.V.H.

DEAR WORLD

A SYRIAN GIRL'S STORY OF WAR AND PLEA FOR PEACE

BANA ALABED

THORNDIKE PRESS
A part of Gale, a Cengage Company

Farmington Hills, Mich • San Francisco • New York • Waterville, Maine
Meriden, Conn • Mason, Ohio • Chicago

LIBRARY OF CONGRESS CIP DATA ON FILE.
CATALOGUING IN PUBLICATION FOR THIS BOOK
IS AVAILABLE FROM THE LIBRARY OF CONGRESS.

ISBN-13: 978-1-4328-4443-1 (hardcover)
ISBN-10: 1-4328-4443-1 (hardcover)

Published in 2017 by arrangement with Simon & Schuster, Inc.

Printed in Mexico
1 2 3 4 5 6 7 21 20 19 18 17

I dedicate my book to every child suffering in a war. You are not alone.

Where there's hope, there's life.
It fills us with fresh courage
and makes us strong again.

ANNE FRANK

AUTHOR'S NOTE

I am so happy that I got to write a book, because I love books and I love to read. I am a good writer because I practice a lot, but I still needed some help writing my book. My mum and my editor, who published this book, helped me to tell my story in English. These are all my memories from

the war — the happy times, the scary times, and everything I could remember. I tried not to forget anything and to tell it right. I hope you like my book. I hope it makes you want to help people.

It was a perfect June day when you came into the world, Bana. Warm, bright, and cloudless. I looked out the window of the hospital room, hands resting on my swollen belly and feeling you kick and squirm as if impatient to be here already, and I thought, There couldn't be a more perfect day for a new life to start. For a minute I forgot about the pain of labor and my fear of what was to come — instead, I thought about how I would soon be sitting in this bed, holding you tightly in my arms, and you would see this same thick sunlight for the first time, feel its warmth on your face; the precious first moments of your beautiful life.

We had waited a long time for you. Not just your father and me but also all of your aunts and uncles and especially your grandparents, who were eager for their first grandchild. When my father arranged my marriage to Baba, our families agreed that we would delay the wedding until I could finish school. And then we wanted to have a little time to be a couple, to get to know each other before we had children. But since Ghassan and I are the oldest in both of our families and the first to be married, everyone was ready for a new little one and for us to start on the next generation. So it was that almost from the very day after our wedding, at every dinner or family visit, someone — especially Grandma Alabed — would inevitably insist, "It's time for a baby."

What they didn't know is that I was having trouble getting pregnant and had to go to many doctors for more than a year. With each month that it didn't happen, I would become more and more terrified that it never would, that I would never get to be a mother. One day, in the middle of this cycle of hope and disappointment, your baba and I were walking around the Citadel of Aleppo, one of my favorite places. The ancient stone walls always made me feel safe and peaceful. Aleppo is one of the oldest continuously inhabited cities in the whole world, Bana. Did you know that? It comforted me to think of that and to feel connected to our history and the ancestors who walked in this very same place over the course of thousands of years.

It was crowded, always, with families and couples, and this day was no different, with many people enjoying an early spring day. That was how it was before the war — so many ordinary days: your father going to work, me visiting with your grandparents and shopping for dinner, helping Grandma Alabed cook, and then taking a stroll after dinner.

It's hard to think about that now. We took it for granted that things would always be like this, with no way to know, or even comprehend, what the future held. It would not have been possible to imagine then that this place where we were walking, which had stood for centuries, would soon be all but destroyed. But all of that was in the future; that day we were happy.

You know your father can be a little quiet sometimes, but he would become animated when he talked about the future. He had just bought a crib. I thought it might be bad luck, since I still wasn't yet pregnant, but your baba is optimistic like that. He proceeds as if the future and his dreams and plans are guaranteed. It's one of the things I love most about him. In those early days of our marriage we would spend hours talking about the lives we wanted to have, which is what we were doing on our walk. Ahead of us, a little girl caught our eye. She must have been about four. She was striking, with long, thick hair and bright gray eyes. We couldn't take our eyes off her as she ran and laughed — my heart filled with such longing that I almost collapsed from the weight of it. Your father turned to me and said that this was the child he pictured for us: a daughter, a little girl with long hair who was filled with energy and laughter. A little girl who would captivate strangers. In that moment, a calm came over me. Somehow I knew I would get pregnant; I knew you would come. And that you would be a little girl whom everyone would love.

There are so few precious possessions we were able to take from Syria — a few old family photos, a copy of our wedding invitation, locks of hair from your and your brothers' first haircuts, and the pregnancy test I took the day I found out I was having you. Even now, when I look down at the faded blue line, it brings back the feeling I had that day — when I was bursting with excitement for the future. When I knew I was finally going to get to be a mother. Your mother. When everything seemed possible and the future was boundless.

Nine months later, when they put you in my arms, you locked your huge brown eyes on mine, and I felt a jolt of love so strong it was as if it were an actual current running through my body. First I prayed to Allah that you would be in good health and that you would have a good spirit. I said my favorite prayer from the Quran: "I seek refuge in the Lord of daybreak, from the evil of that which he created and from the evil of darkness when it settles. And from the evil of the blowers in knots. And from the evil of an envier when he envies." I had repeated this verse out loud to you the whole time I was pregnant because I'd read that you could hear my voice, and I wanted you to be born knowing God. Then I leaned over and whispered my dreams for you in your ear so that those would be the very first words you heard, so that from then on you could carry those whispers in your heart.

Your name means "tree" in Arabic. We chose this because it is a strong name, and we wanted a strong little girl. And you are, Bana — you are strong and you are brave. And wise beyond your years. People call it being an "old soul." You came into the world with a wisdom that everyone around you sensed and was drawn to. It still fills me with pride.

Even as an infant, you were so alert and observed everything around you as though you knew exactly what was going on. You never wanted to sleep, as if you didn't dare miss a moment of anything. When we gathered with all your aunts and uncles at Grandma Alabed's, you seemed to follow the conversation, your bright eyes searching the faces of everyone around you as you were passed from lap to lap and adored. Everyone wanted to play with you or take you for walks, especially your uncle Nezar. We teased him for always wanting to take you to the park or the market because you were so cute that all the pretty girls would want to stop and fawn over you, and he could talk to them.

Do you remember how happy you were to learn to read? You were only three, my clever girl! But your chubby little fingers traced the pages of your favorite books as you bit your lip in concentration and carefully sounded out each word.

This makes me so happy — how curious you are and how eager you have always been to learn — because in this you take after me. I loved school so much. One of my favorite memories from my own childhood was when I was just a little younger than you are now and started school. I was so excited when my mum, your nana Samar, would pick me up for the twenty-minute walk home each day and I could tell her about everything I was learning — that I could write my name and add double-digit numbers and tell time. It felt like I couldn't learn everything I wanted to know fast enough. You are the same way.

When I was teaching you to read, I would

imagine how in a few short years it would be me walking you to school. How I looked forward to that, to the days when you would grab my hand and tell me all about the exciting things you were learning. How we would go over your homework together each night at the table as I made dinner. I never imagined that you wouldn't be able to go to school because the schools would all be destroyed. That instead of sitting at the table doing homework, we would be crouching under it as bombs fell around us. Or that by your fourth birthday, your childhood — the safe, happy, peaceful childhood that every mother dreams of for her children — would descend into a nightmare.

You had three perfect years in Syria, Bana. I hope you never lose those memories from before the war — swimming with Baba at the pool; singing the silly songs you and Yasmin liked to make up; begging us to take you on the Ferris wheel, the air filled with the sweet scent of jasmine from our little garden on the balcony.

I hope the homeland of your early years is imprinted on you and that you understand that wherever you are, the blood of Syria and the pride of our people runs through you. I want for you to hold on to the feeling of being surrounded by your aunts, uncles, and grand-

17

parents, even though we are all scattered now. I want that sense of belonging to be a part of you and to make you feel safe. May the memories of your first happy years of life always live inside you as part of your spirit to sustain you and be a source of hope and courage.

Hold in your heart all that came before, Bana; it was beautiful.

I Was Born with a Smile on My Face.

My mummy told me I was born with a smile on my face. She says that I was always happy, even though I never wanted to sleep because I didn't want to miss anything.

I had many reasons to be happy when I was little. My baba always took me swimming at Alrabea Pool, which was my favorite thing to do. Going to the swings was my second favorite thing to do. I would also go to the market with my uncles to get Jell-O. (Always red, because that is the best flavor.) My family would go to eat at restaurants, and I would get to talk to many different people. Or we would eat dinner all together many nights at Grandma Alabed's house, and there were always a lot of people there because I have so many aunts and uncles and four grandparents and two great-grandmothers. I had many books I loved to read, especially my favorite, *Snow White.* I love all stories about princesses.

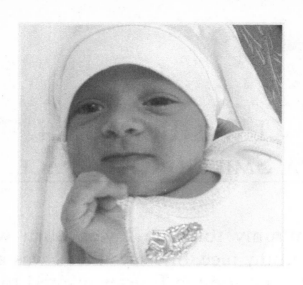

And another big reason to be happy: my baby brother. I prayed that Mummy would have a girl, because I wanted a sister very badly. But my brother was tiny and cute, with thick black hair that was soft like a doll's — so it wasn't so bad that he was a boy. When Mummy was pregnant, I picked out a name for a sister: Warda, which means "flower," because another thing I love is flowers. But you can't call a boy Warda. Instead the name we gave him is Liath (which means "Lion") Mohamed. We call him Mohamed.

I was only three when Mohamed was born, but I took care of him. I would bring Mummy nappies when she needed to change him, share my toys with him, and

say "Shush, shush" when he was crying.

At night I got to hold Mohamed in my lap, and Mum would sit next to us on the sofa in the living room and read to us. Baba would come in and sit in his favorite chair and listen to Mummy read too. When she was done with the story, I would go over and climb into Baba's lap while Mummy put Mohamed to bed. Mum would tell Baba that he should take me to bed too, but we both liked it better when I fell asleep on his chest. He would tell me stories from when he was little and some that he made up. My favorite was the one about a mummy sheep who leaves her babies at home and tells

21

them not to open the door for anyone unless they know the secret word, and then a wolf comes and tricks the babies into thinking he is their mother. They open the door, and the wolf eats the sheep! I hate that part. But the mummy gets the sheep out of the wolf's stomach and puts rocks in there instead.

I could feel Baba's voice through his chest as he told me the stories, and it would make me feel warm inside. The best place to be was in Baba's lap.

So, not many bad things happened to my family. Mummy would say that we are blessed. I thought my family would always be happy.

23

I WANTED TO LIVE
IN SYRIA ALWAYS.

I wanted to live in Syria always because it is a special place. It is a very, very old country, and my family has lived there forever. Grandpa Malek says that it is important to understand where you come from because that makes you who you are. He says we should be proud to be Syrians, because Syrians are kind and honest. You can leave a million pounds in your house and no one will steal it. We always share whatever we have with our neighbors and take care of our families, because family is the most important thing to us. We know that we should always be generous and loyal and true to Allah. We pray a lot so that God will help us be good. We want a simple life. This is what is important to us.

When Grandpa was a little boy, he lived in the countryside. When he grew up he married Nana Samar, who grew up in Aleppo, so they moved there even though

Grandpa always said he liked the country better because it is more quiet and there is fresh air. Mummy and all her brothers and sisters were born in Aleppo. And Baba and his brothers and sister were too. I was born in Aleppo also, just like them. When I grew up, I was going to live down the street from my best friends, Yasmin and Fatemah, and from Mummy and Baba, just like they live down the street from their parents. My family and I could eat dinner together all the time and go for walks at the Citadel of Aleppo and make each other laugh. Everyone in my family liked to laugh, so that was easy. I was going to become a teacher and teach Syrian children how to speak English.

Those were my dreams.

NOTHING HELPED US TO FORGET BABA WASN'T THERE.

Then the bad times started. First they came to take Baba away. Mummy, Mohamed, and I were at Grandma Alabed's house. Baba and his brothers were down the street sitting in front of the market like usual. They were there almost every evening, sitting in folding chairs, drinking apple tea, and laughing about funny memories or arguing about who was better at PlayStation or who was smarter and more successful using loud voices, even though nobody was actually mad. Baba and all his brothers grew up in our neighborhood, so all their friends would come around too. Mummy said they liked to pretend they were still teenagers. Sometimes I got to sit with them, and they would tease me about how I thought I was all grown up even though I was little.

This day, Uncle Nezar came running to Grandma Alabed's house, where Mummy, Grandma, and I were making dinner, and

26

told us they took Baba away. "They" is the *Mukhābarāt,* the secret police who work for the president of Syria, Bashar al-Assad.

I asked Mum why Baba wasn't coming home and where Baba went and when he would be back.

"He'll be home soon, Bon Bon," she said, and gave me a hug. "Some people just need to ask him some questions. Everything will be fine."

But I didn't know whether that was true, because everyone seemed very worried. No one even wanted to eat the dinner we made. All the uncles stayed in the living room talking about how the police took Baba because the regime thinks everyone is a spy — especially the men. They have to question people to find out who is loyal. My baba was not a spy, he was a lawyer; it was his job to help people and to make sure things were fair.

We stayed over at Grandma's house that night because it was too sad to go home without Baba. It was better to all be at Grandma's and worry about Baba together. All the next day, Baba still did not come back. We didn't know where he was. We tried to sing songs. We tried to color. We tried to read, but nothing helped us forget that Baba was not there. Mohamed kept

27

crying for Baba, because Baba had never been gone before. I kept telling him what Mummy had told me: "He'll be home soon." That night Mummy prayed with me. We asked if God would please make it so that Baba could return soon.

It worked! The next day Baba came home. He looked tired and smelt bad, but we hugged him anyway. He said: "I'm fine. It's going to be okay."

But it wasn't okay, because soon the bombs came.

"Are You Okay? Are You Okay? Are You Okay?"

I didn't know what it was when the first big bomb came. It was just a regular day; I was at Nana Samar and Grandpa Malek's house with Mohamed. They watched us during the day while Mummy went to school and Baba went to work. Mummy loved university and was studying to be a lawyer like Baba. I liked to pretend I went to the university too and colored in my notebooks for my homework.

I was sitting on the floor playing with my dolls. I had two favorites: one was tall like me and wore a uniform because she went to school, and the other was a baby in a pink dress. Mohamed was crawling around next to me, and he would always laugh when I made my dolls talk in a funny voice, which is what I was doing when suddenly there was a **BOOM!** It was the loudest noise I had ever heard in my life, a noise so big you could feel it in your body, not just

29

hear it. The sound and the surprise made my body feel like jelly.

We didn't know what to do, because we didn't know what was happening. Mohamed started to cry, and Nana Samar ran in from the kitchen. "Come, come! Get away from the glass!" We all ran to the kitchen where there were no windows. I asked Nana what made the loud noise and why we had to run. She said that a bomb had fallen somewhere in Aleppo.

"What's a bomb?" I asked her. She told me it was something that blows things up.

I had a scary thought: What if it blew Mummy and Baba up? I kept trying to get that thought to go away, but it wouldn't. I felt like my insides were shaking and I wanted to cry, but I didn't. Mum always told me I was brave and strong even before the war. She said God made me this way. I was lucky He did, because there would be many times I would need to be strong that I didn't even know about yet.

After a little while we heard the front door open, and Mummy came running into the kitchen and grabbed us. "Are you okay? Are you okay? Are you okay?" she asked over and over while she hugged and kissed us. I was okay, but when I saw Mummy I started to cry because I was scared and also so happy at the same time that she was there. She called Baba at work. He was okay and would be there soon. I could feel Mummy's heart beating through her chest when she hugged me. "I was so worried about you," she said. Mummy was very brave like me, even though she was scared also. You can be both. I know, because it happened to me a lot starting that day.

Nana Samar hugged Mummy too — she always said Mummy was her "baby girl" even though Mummy is grown up. She told us that we had better "make preparations" and that Mummy should go to the roof and get my baby pool so they could collect water in it in case there was no more water.

As soon as Mummy left to go to the roof, another bomb exploded — even bigger and louder. This time I screamed. I didn't even mean to — the yell just came out. Mummy ran back downstairs and hugged me. Nana Samar grabbed Grandpa Malek's hand and said: "Oh God. What are we going to do?" But no one answered.

From then on, every day it was bombing, bombing, bombing. Giant planes would fly across the sky and drop bombs here and there, wherever they felt like it. Sometimes a plane flew so low that we could see the pilot. Did he know that he was hurting and

31

killing people? He must have, but how could he do that?

I asked Mummy, but she didn't know. I asked her other questions too, like why people wanted to hurt us with guns and bombs. I didn't understand why there was fighting. Every time I asked Mummy these questions, she would just hug me and tell me not to worry. She said that we had to pray that the fighting would stop soon and that we would stay safe.

So I started to pray every night before bed: "Please stop the war." I wanted things to be like they used to be. One night, Mummy heard my prayers and said, "It won't always be like this, Bana." I could tell she was sad too.

She said, "This will all be over soon."

But it wasn't.

WE ALL KNEW WHAT TO DO WHEN WE HEARD THE BOMBS.

If you haven't been in a war, you might think there is only one type of bomb. But there are actually many different kinds. I learned about all of them quickly because I am a fast learner. One way you can tell the difference between bombs is by how they sound.

One has a long, high squeal like a whistle and then a big boom.

One is like a car engine revving, *vroom, vroom,* and then boom.

One is like *bap, bap, bap* all the way down. This is a cluster bomb, which is like a big bomb with many smaller bombs in it, and sharp parts go everywhere when it hits.

One is quiet — there is almost no noise, and then, when the boom comes, it lights up the sky bright yellow. The stuff that makes the sky light up is called phosphorous. One time I woke up and went to get Mummy to wake up too, since it was morning. But Mummy said it was still the middle of the night. I told her I could see the sun through the window; it was light outside. But that was just the phosphorous.

A chlorine bomb is the worst. You need chlorine in a pool to keep the water clean, and it never bothered me when I went swimming. But in the air it stings your eyes so badly that you have so many tears even if you're not crying.

We all knew what to do when we heard the bombs: if they were far away, run to the room in our house that has no windows that Mummy used to store old clothes and things to clean the house. If they were close, run to the basement, or at least down to Uncle Wesam's on the first floor.

Even if we were in the middle of eating dinner, as soon as we heard the rumble of the planes, we got up and left our food and ran down the two flights of stairs to the basement of our building. Our building had four floors: we lived on the second floor, and my uncles Wesam, Mazen, and Nezar and their families lived on the other floors. I liked that all of us got to live together in the same building, especially my cousin Lana, because she was more like the younger sister I always wanted than a cousin.

And since we all lived in one building, we

could all run down to the basement together. There were two basements in the
building. Both of them were dark and cold,
with gray cement walls and old tools and
boxes. There was no electricity; sometimes
we had a flashlight, but a lot of the time we
would just have to sit in the dark. I hated
the basement. But it was safer than being in
our apartment. Sometimes we had to stay
down there for hours waiting for the bombing to stop. Then our food was cold, and no
one wanted to eat it. We would clean up
and go to bed. And I would pray some more.

We Had to Try to Forget the War and Be Normal.

Eid al-Fitr is my favorite holiday. It is when Muslims celebrate the end of Ramadan. Ramadan is when grown-ups fast during the day for one whole month. Then, at the end of the month, you celebrate that it is over with Eid. It's a fun holiday — or it used to be before the war. For Eid, you clean the house so that everything sparkles and smells good. And you get new clothes and shoes — the stores even stay open all night so you can buy things. Then you have a big feast, with so much food that you eat and eat until your stomach hurts. And you do special prayers.

We were at Grandma and Grandpa Al-abed's new house to celebrate Eid. I didn't like it as much as their old house. Their old apartment was very big, so we could run around, and it had a treadmill, which was fun to walk on, and a huge balcony. I had lots of dolls that lived there, and they liked it better too. The best part, though, was that it was close to us in East Aleppo, and I would walk to their house almost every day. But when the regime's army started bombing East Aleppo, Grandma got scared of the bombs and loud noises and decided to get an apartment in West Aleppo. It was safer there, because that's where many of the people who worked for or supported the government lived. It used to be that Aleppo was one city, but now it was divided into east and west. In between it was especially dangerous, because that was where the Free Syrian Army was fighting the regime. There were many soldiers and guns, and people were killed there almost every day.

After our Eid feast everyone was in a good mood, even though there was war. Mummy always reminded us that we had to try to forget the bombs and be normal, and sometimes it worked. Lana and I were playing dress-up in the new clothes we'd gotten for Eid. I was pretending to be my favorite princess — Rapunzel. I want my hair to be as long as hers, so I will never cut it. I heard Mummy get a call from Nana Samar. Mummy's younger sister, my aunt Eman, had been shot. She had finished her exams at the university and was in a car going to Nana Samar's for Eid. She was shot by a

government helicopter that was firing guns down on any cars trying to cross from West to East Aleppo. Bullets had hit Aunt Eman's leg, and she had to go to the hospital. I was scared for her. I bet her leg was bleeding a lot. I really wanted to see Auntie and give her a hug, but she was too far away, and it was too dangerous to cross back to the east side. We only risked it sometimes to see Grandma Alabed, and only in the daytime after we looked to see whether there was a lot of fighting that day. Even still, it was always scary. You never knew what could happen.

They had taken Aunt Eman to a hospital in the countryside because it was safer, and because many hospitals in East Aleppo had been bombed and didn't work anymore. Aunt Eman had to stay at the hospital for two weeks before she came home. I was glad to finally give her a big hug when she came back to Nana's house, but I didn't like to see the dark red scars like fat worms on her leg. Grandpa Malek said Aunt Eman was "good as new."

"What If They Are Dead?"

Then there were more bad times. My uncles Mazen and Yaman disappeared one day. They went out in the morning to get breakfast and never came home. We were very worried that the *Mukhābarāt* had taken them the way they had taken Baba. But then Baba got a call, and the man on the phone said he had my uncles and we would have to pay to get them back.

All my uncles came over and talked in rushed voices, trying to figure out what to do. The kidnappers wanted more money than we had. Baba called the man back and asked him if they would take less. Baba was in charge because he is the oldest, like I am the oldest. So he had to talk to the kidnappers and make a deal. Then Grandpa Malek drove Uncle Wesam to deliver the money. They were supposed to leave it in a certain rubbish bin on Castello Road.

"Be careful," everyone told Uncle Wesam.

Grandma Alabed was especially worried and barely wanted to let him go when she hugged him before he left. We were nervous that the men could be tricking us and would take the money but wouldn't give Uncles Mazen and Yaman back.

Grandma Alabed cried and cried and said, "What if they are dead?" I promised her they weren't dead. I put my head in her lap and said, "Everything will be okay." That's what Mum always told me.

I was right! They were alive. We had to wait all day, but before it was dark, they came home! They looked tired and sad, like when Baba came home from being gone with the men. But at least no one hurt them. The men who kidnapped them had blindfolds on them the whole time, so we never knew who it was.

After this, Grandpa Malek said it was getting too dangerous. In the war you have to pick a side, especially if you're a boy. You have to fight for the regime, or they will assume you are a rebel and the *Mukhābarāt* will take you away. So Grandpa Malek said it was time for Mummy's younger brothers Maher and Ahmad to go away. This gave me a terrible feeling inside. I loved my uncles, because they gave me sweets and always said that I am more like their little sister than their niece. They were now going far away to Egypt to go to school.

We all went over to Nana Samar's to say good-bye. I couldn't believe they had to leave. I was going to miss them so much. "I don't want you to go. I want you to stay with us," I told them. They said, "We don't want to go either." I ran outside after them when they got into the car. I ran behind the car all the way down the street. I could hear Mummy calling for me to come back, and my legs were burning from running so fast to try to keep up. I was so out of breath! But I didn't stop. Uncle Maher waved out the window the whole time. Right before I almost couldn't see the car anymore I could hear them calling, "We'll see you soon, Bon Bon!"

But I never saw them again.

"STOP SHOOTING AT US!"

After a while I started to almost get used to the bombs. But there were other scary things besides bombs, like the time Mummy and I were at Grandma and Grandpa Al-abed's house for Eid al-Adha. This holiday is a few weeks after Eid al-Fitr and cele-brates the end of the Hajj, when Muslims go to Mecca, which is a holy place. The holi-est. That means you can feel close to God there. All Muslims are supposed to do a Hajj once in their lives if they can. Mummy did hers when she was sixteen.

We were staying at Grandma's house for a whole week. Baba couldn't come with us the first night because he was helping Uncle Wesam at his clothing store; it was extra busy for Eid, with people buying new clothes to celebrate. I'd gotten a brand-new pair of pink Barbie boots with sparkles on them. I was wearing them all day, I loved them so much. I begged Mummy to let me sleep in them, but she said I had to take them off when I went to bed. I put them right next to me so I could put them on as soon as I woke up in the morning.

I was sleeping when a very loud **bap-bap-bap-bap** suddenly woke me up. I knew that sound: guns. Lana and Mohamed woke up too, and I told them there were soldiers outside fighting. All the grown-ups were up now, and everyone was running through the apartment screaming and trying to figure out what was going on, why the soldiers had surrounded Grandma's building and were shooting at it.

It was too dangerous to go near the windows because there was so much shooting. We also heard grenades — bombs you throw with your hands instead of dropping from a plane — exploding all around the building. We opened the door to the hallway, and the neighbors were also screaming and crying over the sounds of the guns firing and the soldiers yelling. "What is that? What's happening? Why are they shooting at the building?" everyone yelled, scared.

We all decided to run down to the basement as fast as we could. We were wearing only our pajamas, and it was cold in the basement. We had to run out so fast that I didn't have time to put on my new Barbie boots. I wished I had slept in them like I wanted to.

All the neighbors huddled with their families to keep warm. Hours and hours passed, and still all we heard was guns firing and men yelling. We were getting so tired and hungry. We had no food or water.

One of the little boys kept crying that he was hungry. I wondered if he wasn't used to the basement and having to run there all the time because he lived in West Aleppo. Mohamed and I knew how to be good and patient and quiet in the basement.

The little boy's father talked with my uncles and some other people and decided to go to the top of the stairs and yell for the soldiers to please let us leave the building, that we needed to get food and water for the children.

We could hear him screaming, "Stop shooting at us! We are civilians. This is our home. Let us go!"

I couldn't believe the soldiers could hear him over the guns, but one yelled back, "Fine, get out now. NOW! You have five minutes."

Mummy grabbed me and Mohamed, and we all ran up the stairs from the basement and went outside. We stayed close to the building, like we were hiding. And we ran as fast as we could, like we were in a race. It was almost dark by now, and it was even colder outside than it was in the basement. I was shivering in my thin pajamas and bare feet.

We ran over to the building next door, and the people who lived there welcomed us in. They gave us blankets and some water. Water tastes so good when you haven't had it in a long time. It also feels good going down your dry throat and when you can feel it in your stomach. I could feel it when it got to my stomach because it was so empty after going a whole day with nothing to eat.

One of my uncles went to ask other people in the building what was happening. He came back and told us that there was an important man who worked for the regime living in Grandma's building. The rebels had surrounded the building to try to get him.

After a few more hours it was fully dark, and everything became quiet. It had started pouring rain outside. The soldiers went home, so we could too. We called Grandpa Malek to pick us up. We had only one car, and it was dangerous to cross to East Aleppo even once, so we couldn't make many trips. We had to fit eleven family members in the car — four men, four women, and three children. I don't know how we did that. We were all soaking wet and freezing cold. I felt bad for Mohamed because he smelt very bad and was crying a lot because his nappy was so dirty; he hadn't had a new one for a whole day. It seemed like the happy time of Eid dinner was so long ago that we could barely remember it.

Baba was so worried about us when we got home and told him everything that had happened. He said he would help Grandma and Grandpa find another new place to live. Grandma said that maybe it was time for her and Grandpa to make a plan to leave Syria. And then she cried a lot.

There Was Nowhere That Was Safe Anymore.

A few days later, Grandpa Malek drove us back to Grandma Alabed's house to get everything that we had had to leave behind when we had to run out. I wanted to come so I could get my Barbie boots. When we pulled up to park in front of the apartment building, Grandpa Malek said, "We must get in and out as fast as we can."

But when we went into the building, there were soldiers from the regime inside. They were in Grandma and Grandpa's apartment like it was theirs. They held guns that were bigger than Mohamed. They were angry and started yelling. One man had ugly yellow teeth, and spit came out of his mouth when he talked. He said that one of us must have told the rebels that his friend lived in the building.

But none of us had done that, because we didn't even know he lived there.

The man didn't believe us. He said that

all the men in our family must be working for the rebels. He told Mummy that she had to call Baba and her other brothers and tell them to come now, or they would go find them. He asked for our address.

I was scared because he didn't believe us. Baba was at home with Mohamed, and if they took Baba away, who would stay with Mohamed? Or would they take Mohamed too? I didn't know.

The man said to the grown-ups, "Give me your phones now!"

Mummy said she didn't bring her phone. Then she suddenly said, "I need to take Bana to the bathroom," even though I didn't have to go.

When we went to the bathroom, Mummy said, "Shh, shh," and pulled out her phone. She had hidden it under her clothes. That was very clever. You're not supposed to lie, but this time it was okay.

She called Baba and whispered, "Ghassan, the regime army is here. They want to take all the men. If something happens to us, it is the regime. I love you." And then she hung up. We flushed the toilet even though I hadn't used it. I didn't want to leave the bathroom. What if the soldiers decided to shoot us?

Mummy squeezed my hand, and that

made me feel a little better.

We went back out to the living room, and the soldiers kept us there for four more hours before they finally told us we could leave, but they said we could never come back. We tried to gather Grandma's stuff as quickly as we could, but the soldiers had already taken most of it — her computer and TV and sheets and towels and clothes. Luckily, my new Barbie boots were still there, but I felt bad being happy about that, since Grandma Alabed was so sad. She cried some more. It felt like Grandma Alabed was always crying, and I didn't know how to make her feel better anymore. Grandma and Grandpa didn't have any place to go. It was too dangerous in East Aleppo, and we weren't allowed in West Aleppo ever again.

There was nowhere that was safe anymore.

I Hated the War.

Before the big bombs came, sometimes I would go to Nana Samar and Grandpa Malek's house, and sometimes I got to go to school for a few days a week. I was learning about letters and colors and was reading many new books. I was always excited to go.

One morning I got out of bed like usual to find Mummy so I could get dressed. But as soon as I got up a bomb went off, and it was very close. I fell to the ground and covered my ears. There was a boom and then a big crack, like clapping but so much louder. It was all the glass in the windows breaking. A million pieces of sharp glass fell right onto the bed where I had just been sleeping.

Mummy screamed my name and grabbed me. Her face turned white like a cloud. I told her I was okay. Baba hugged both of us extra tight, and then he left to go find my

uncles so that they could fix the glass. I wished they could fix the war.

I didn't cry when I heard the bomb, but I did cry later when Baba and Mummy decided that I couldn't go to school anymore. It wasn't safe, because a bomb could fall on the school. The regime does not like schools, so they bombed them a lot.

I had to stop going swimming and to the park too. I was almost getting to be a really good swimmer until I couldn't go anymore. I also couldn't play outside with my best friend, Yasmin, because a big bomb might fall on us. Mummy stopped going to the university because it was too dangerous. I always felt a lump in my throat when I thought about how we couldn't do any of the things we loved anymore. I hated the war.

It was my job to protect you, Bana. For every mother, it is her highest priority to keep her children safe. The day the first large bombs started falling in Aleppo in the summer of 2012 came a sickening moment when I realized just how hard this would be. It was the first time I had faced this helplessness — a feeling I would experience time and time again.

It had been a good day — we had final exams, and I was pleased to feel so confident in all my answers; my late evenings of studying the previous week after I put you and Mohamed to bed had paid off. I was excelling and enjoying my courses, and with two years to go to get my law degree, I was already envisioning my career. You know how much I love to teach — I thought I would become a law school professor so I could combine two of my greatest passions.

Periodically throughout the test, the other students and I heard the rumblings of small bombs — distant distractions we did our best to ignore. We'd had some practice at it by this time. It's funny that at one point the bombs were background noise that we could tune out like birds or rain. But that day, the scale of the war changed when the planes came and the air offensive began in Aleppo.

After the exam, I was on the bus to pick you up from Nana's when the sky exploded. It was hard to comprehend what was happening — it was as if some other new reality had suddenly emerged, but I was stuck five minutes before when the world had made more sense, when I was thinking about what to make for dinner. It felt like I couldn't catch up to the new situation, in which bombs fell from the sky. It's a cliché, but it was like a bad movie, or a surreal nightmare. It felt . . . unbelievable.

The other people on the bus looked stricken and confused, as I'm sure I did as well. Sometimes in life we have moments when there is before and then there is after, and you understand those two lives are going to be completely different. This was like that. The woman sitting across the aisle from me began to pray, silently and urgently.

When the bus crossed the al-Sha'ar bridge, we could see a huge cloud of black smoke a few miles away. I could tell it was near your grandmother's house, where you were, and panic overwhelmed me. I had heard the expression "take your breath away," but I never knew that it could literally happen. I felt like there was no air in my body, that my lungs had just stopped working. Later I would become all too familiar with this feeling, but that day it was a stranger to me still. I had never really known fear in my life.

The thirty-minute journey to get to your grandmother's was the longest of my life. To have to wonder for even one second if harm has befallen your children is a particular torture. This was still before I carried a mobile phone everywhere — that's probably hard for you to even imagine — so I didn't even have a way to get in touch with your father or your grandparents to find out if everyone was okay. All I could do was wait and worry.

So when I finally made it to Nana's house and held you and Mohamed in my arms, to know that at least for the moment you were safe, alive — well, it was a moment of happiness more pure even than that I had felt when both of you were born. It was a happiness born of relief that my worst nightmare hadn't come true. But it was short-lived, because another bomb shattered the moment. And so it began.

We probably should have been more prepared for that day, for the war to arrive in Aleppo. The seeds had been sown years before. We had followed all the fighting and turmoil in other countries during the Arab Spring. Governments fell and leaders were deposed and killed elsewhere, but it seemed so far away. We thought something like that would never happen here. I suppose that's what everyone believes until it is too late.

But in Syria, at that time, life was good, peaceful overall. If you were like our family, at least, middle-class and educated, there were opportunities, and you could build a good life for your family, as my parents did for me, and theirs had before them, and so on as far back as you could remember. A long, happy life in Syria was your birthright, Bana, and you have been robbed of that.

Even when the violence began in our country — the uprising in Daraa in 2011 when the teenagers were arrested and brutally beaten and tortured by the regime for spray-painting anti-Assad graffiti on their school — we were shocked and appalled, but it still felt far away. It was tragic but distant, as so many people's troubles are. We didn't feel a lot of opposition in Aleppo, and we were convinced that these skirmishes and rebellions would fizzle out or be resolved or stay contained.

Yes, I was frantic when the regime took your

father away. It was the first time that the unrest had come to our doorstep, and I had heard the horror stories of what they were capable of — the forms of torture you can't even imagine. But your father and I were not political people — we were not for or against — we just wanted to work hard and provide for our family. I knew that Ghassan had done nothing that would draw concern. Even though those were the longest hours of my life, imagining and preparing for the worst, I still believed that your father would be okay, that he would come home to us. The alternative — that we would never see him again — was incomprehensible, even though it happened to wives all over Syria — their husbands just abruptly disappeared.

For me, optimism was a weapon against fear and despair. I tended to my hope from that point forward like it was a fire that I couldn't let go out. Against all odds, your father and I somehow believed — forced ourselves to believe — that we would be spared. The human impulse for optimism is our greatest strength and our biggest liability.

Because in actuality the war was like a distant ocean wave, gathering strength and force so that by the time it crested over Aleppo it was a tsunami that crashed into us with a momentum and intensity that blindsided us, exploding into our lives that day when I was on my way home from the university. There was before that and after that — a razor-thin edge drawn by fate.

We had no way of knowing just how bad it would get. If we had understood from the beginning how things would end up in Aleppo or the horrors that awaited us, we would have left. So many people did, at least in the early days when you still could. Some fared well, but we also heard the terrible stories of isolation and poverty and then worse, as people ended up living in camps or died trying to cross dangerous seas and deserts to get to countries that didn't want them there.

It is a hard thing to leave your entire life and everything you've ever known and become a refugee. The bombs were terrifying, yes, but the idea of starting over with nothing was equally harrowing. Even if we were able to do so logistically, just what sort of life would we have? How was your father supposed to work? How would we have money? How would we have friends? Would you be able to go to school? War had made our lives terrible, but the unknown was just as scary.

There is a Syrian proverb: The weeds of your own country are better than the wheat of a stranger's. That explains how tied we felt to our homeland, and how loyal. And we loved our little home too, Bana, the one your baba and I built and filled with love and so many memories and special things. Even the air-conditioning had sentimental value. Did I ever tell you the story of the A/C? No one in our family had ever had air-conditioning. Even in the summers, when temperatures could become blistering, we had always made do; air-conditioning was something of a luxury. Well, when we brought you home from the hospital on that warm June afternoon, your father worried that you would be too hot in our apartment and suddenly ran out to get an air conditioner, which he installed in your nursery. I laughed at him as he struggled and sweated to get it in the window. I told him that we'd always been fine without A/C, and you would be too. But he insisted. "I want our little girl to be comfortable," he told me, looking down at you like you were the most precious thing in the world. Which, of course, you were.

It's such a little thing, a silly thing maybe, but to me that A/C became a symbol of your father's love for you and the lengths to which he would go to make sure you were always happy, safe, and comfortable. And there were other things too — your clothes and books and dolls and all the luxuries your father and I saved up to buy. Like the television set we saved for for five months and could finally afford after Baba won his first big case. We felt like such grown-ups when we bought that TV! These are just "things," I understand that, and things can be replaced. And yet things can matter, Bana. They are the objects, lovingly collected, that make up a home, and a home is where you feel safe and loved. That matters. A lot. More than anything.

So our choice — stay or go — was between two evils. That is, when we had a choice at all. Because before we knew it, there came a point of no return, and we were trapped; it became impossible to leave.

Not a day goes by that I don't think of what we would have been spared — especially the nightmare of the last two weeks in Syria — if we had left. Was it pride that made us stay? Or fear? Denial? Possibly it was all of that. But mainly it was stubborn hope — a hope that was fueled when things periodically got better, when the bombing stopped for days or even months at a time and we would get an exquisite taste of normalcy.

Also, because we had some savings, we were lucky enough to be able to cope with the hardships of war in a way some other families could not. We were able to buy a generator and solar panels, and to stockpile food. With these things, we felt like we could hunker down and weather the storm until things got better.

But always, always the bombs would come again, and they would be even worse than before. The fear and despair would come crashing back even worse than before too, because we dared allow ourselves to believe it would be different this time, that the war would eventually end. It reminded us that our hope was as fragile as the first blooms of jasmine in our garden, and as easily crushed.

Mothers feel guilty about so much. You will see when you have your own children — you are always filled with worry. I laugh when I think about the things I was up at night fretting about before the war. I worried every time you sneezed or had a slight cough. Were you eating too many sweets? How much TV should I let you watch? What I wouldn't have given for those to have remained my greatest concerns. To worry about what you ate, and not whether you would even have any food to eat. To worry about a little cold, and not you getting hit by a bullet or shrapnel.

These days, if I let it — and sometimes I can't help it — my guilt will tear through me. What more could I have done to shield you? Will you be scarred, and how could I have prevented that? Did the trauma you've experienced imprint itself on you? Are there two versions of you — the one you would have been if you had grown up in peace, and the girl you are now, shaped by war?

It is hard to describe the relentless toll living in fear for your life all the time takes on you. It is a feeling you know all too well, little one. You've seen more death and destruction in your short life than most adults have ever seen, and Baba and I were not able to protect you from that. I tried to hide my fear from you as much as possible so that you wouldn't be afraid.

And I tried to keep things as "normal" as possible for you, Bana — even during those awful times. I wanted to make sure your physical body was safe, of course, but I also wanted to make sure your spirit was protected: that you were able to know and understand that even with all the horror, there was still beauty in the world. That we could create beauty in the world, or at the very least in our home and family, and shield ourselves with that.

I tried to make sure you understood that war may have brought out the worst in people, but it also brought out the best and made us grateful for every happy moment.

You may carry some scars, Bana, from all you have seen and experienced, but you also carry a strength of spirit that was forged by growing up in war. You have learned to nurture optimism and a sense of resilience, without which you would have given up. This is the most important and hardest-won lesson you have learned in your young life — that you must never give up on hope, Bana. Or give in to despair. Even if that seems like the only option.

If there is any solace to be had, it is that this lesson and others you have learned in war have strengthened your character and given you perspective. I believe your experiences, however much I may have wanted to spare you from them, have made you that much more generous and grateful, thoughtful and forgiving. Because you've seen the alternative. You've seen the worst, and you've been your best. And that is something, Bana. That is everything.

I Prayed for a Girl.

War is scary, because you are always waiting for bad news — what got ruined or who is leaving or who got hurt or what you can't do anymore because of the bombs (like go to the park). But then there can be a surprise — good news! Like when Mummy told me she was going to have another baby!

I had prayed a lot for Mohamed to come because I wanted a sister. But I didn't pray for this baby because I was busy asking God for the war to be over — still, we were getting one anyway. I was excited, but I was also a little worried about how scared the baby would be with the bombs. Mohamed and I were big enough to run to the basement. But the baby would be tiny.

Sometimes we didn't know how long we would have to stay in the basement. Sometimes it was a few hours, but other times it was many days at a time. So we always had to remember to grab enough food and water and blankets when the bombs came. Mummy would grab a bag that had our valuables and her Quran. I would try to remember to grab one doll and one book if I could, which was all I could carry. Now we would have to remember to grab the baby too.

I told Mummy how happy I was for a new baby and promised to help her just like I had with Mohamed — and even more, because I was bigger now. I asked if she thought the baby would be scared of the bombs or brave.

Her eyes looked shiny, and she said, "We will have to help him be brave."

"Him? It's a boy?" I asked. I was disappointed, because I still wanted a sister. Mummy said she actually didn't know if the baby was a boy or a girl and that it would be a surprise. That was fine, because I like surprises. But still I prayed for a girl, with blond hair, like my doll's.

As Mummy's belly was growing, there weren't as many bombs. This was how it was for a while — sometimes a lot of bombs, and sometimes not very many. A good day was when you heard only three or four bombs, and they were far away. A bad day was when you heard ten bombs and they were close. Sometimes there were so many good days in a row that you forgot there was war. Sometimes we could even go to the park. You had to step over a lot of rubble, and the park was dirty and dusty, but it was still fun. Yasmin and I would clear away a flat part so we could practice skipping rope. Or sometimes we would play hopscotch.

Mummy was tired while she was growing the baby, so I was extra helpful. We always had to make sure that we had enough water every day. Before the war, water would come from the sink, but the bombs broke the water and the power, or sometimes the government would turn off the electricity that pumps the water when they were mad. Sometimes we wouldn't have water for a long time, so we had to store a lot in jugs and use it carefully.

You didn't always know when the water was going to come on or how long it was going to be on. Sometimes a neighbor would alert everyone by going through the streets shouting, "There is water!" Even if it was the middle of the night, you had to get up and get water, since you didn't know when it would be back. Baba and I would go fill water jugs at the huge water tanks in the street. Sometimes we would have to wait in a long line to fill our jugs. They were very

heavy to carry back, but Baba and Uncle Wesam would say, "Almost there, Bon Bon, come on." Once we finally made it back to our building, my arms would be so tired and feel all shaky.

Sometimes if there was no water near us, we would have to drive far away to get it, and we would take a giant metal box and try to get as much water as we could. Getting water was a lot of work, but you can't live without water.

Baba put big panels on the roof that turned the sun into electricity so he and Mummy could charge their phones and Mohamed and I could have TV. We could watch only one hour a day, though. Most days I picked what show we would watch, but I remembered to let Mohamed pick sometimes. He always wanted to watch *SpongeBob SquarePants* or Tom and Jerry cartoons. I thought these shows were kind of silly, but Mohamed needed to forget the war too.

"It's Time to Leave."

Finally, it was time for the baby to arrive, which was good, because I was tired of waiting. But there was a problem. The regime kept blowing up the hospitals in East Aleppo, so there was no place for the baby to be born or doctors to help the baby come. The few doctors there were busy helping the people who were blown up by the bombs. It was getting bad again.

Mummy and Baba were worried. They tried to pretend they weren't, but I could tell they were because Mummy was distracted a lot and sometimes was very quiet. Some babies had been born sick because of the war. I was supposed to have a baby cousin, but he wasn't born because he didn't have any bones. There wasn't enough food, and there were so many bad chemicals and dust in the air all the time that made it smell like metal and burning oil.

Also, when you're scared all the time, it

isn't good for babies, and they don't grow. That's why Mum said we had to be calm and happy when she was growing our baby. We read to Mummy's stomach. I read books I thought the baby would like, like *The Greedy Fox,* and Mummy read the Quran. We wanted the baby to come into the world smiling like me and knowing that God loves him. (Or her!)

But now that the bombs were getting bad again, I was scared about how the baby would come out.

One day when Mummy's stomach was so big that she could barely move, shells from a bomb hit Nana Samar and Grandpa Malek's building right down the street. We were in the basement because the bombing was so close, and when we came upstairs we were scared. You never knew who had died when you came upstairs, or what had been destroyed.

This time, it was very bad. Grandpa's building had two floors. They lived downstairs, and a nice man called Abdo paid Grandpa to live upstairs with his family. The shells from the bomb hit Abdo and hurt him very badly. Grandpa said it could have easily been him who got hit or Nana or any of my aunts and uncles who lived there.

Grandpa sat in our living room and

hugged Nana, who was crying, and he said, "We can't do this anymore."

Everyone was so serious, so I was thinking of how I could make them laugh. Then Grandpa said, "It's time to leave. We can pack tomorrow and get everything in order and leave first thing the following morning."

I forgot about making everyone laugh. My stomach flip-flopped.

I lay down next to Grandpa on the sofa and put my head in his lap. "Please don't go," I said. Grandpa just stroked my hair.

"We're just going to go to Turkey, Bon Bon. Just for a little bit. Until it's better here."

He looked up at Mummy and Baba. "You should come too. It's not safe to stay here. It's getting worse."

My stomach flipped again, because I didn't want to leave Syria.

Mummy and Baba were quiet. I knew that they didn't want to leave either. But if everyone left, then it wouldn't be as fun to stay. And Nana Samar was supposed to help me help Mummy with the baby. Now they wouldn't even meet him! At least Grandma and Grandpa Alabed were still here to help.

While Mummy stayed home to rest, the rest of us went to go help Nana and

Grandpa see what they could pack. We picked what we could out of all the broken pieces of floor and walls. I didn't have to take baths very often, since we had to save water, but that night I did because I was covered in dust.

Mummy and Baba were up late talking. I was supposed to be asleep, but I heard their serious voices. I couldn't sleep, because the next day I knew we would have to say good-bye to Nana and Grandpa, and I was afraid I would never see them again.

"Don't Cry, Bon Bon, I Will See You Soon."

In the early morning the bombs were back again. Every morning we woke to bombs like birds calling.

We ran to the basement. Since Mummy's stomach was so big with the baby, she wasn't as fast, and I worried about that. Before we even got to the basement there was a loud crash. Glass was breaking everywhere. We didn't even stop to see where or what it was, though — we just kept running downstairs.

But Mummy was shaky. She looked very tired and pale. She lay with Baba on the floor of the basement and cried. Mummy didn't cry very much at all, but when she did, I always did too, automatically, like our tears were the same. The worst feeling in the world is when Mummy is upset. I laid my head on her belly and listened to the baby swim around. That made me feel calmer.

When the bombing stopped, we went upstairs and saw that the windows in the living room had been blown out again. We all helped to pick the pieces of glass off the floor. This was the fifth time this had happened; we couldn't get any glass anymore, so Baba put up nylon instead of windows.

Nana and Grandpa came over later that night to say good-bye. But it wasn't going to be good-bye after all, because Mummy and Baba had a new plan. Mummy decided it was just too dangerous to stay in Syria to have the baby after all. So she and Mohamed and I would go with Nana and Grandpa and Aunt Nouran and Uncle Saleh and Grandpa's mother to Turkey.

This was good news, because I didn't have to say good-bye to them. But it was also bad news, because Baba wasn't coming with us. He was going to stay behind and keep our house safe so that no one came in and took our stuff because they thought we had gone forever. He believed we would be back from Turkey very soon because the war would be better. In the meantime, he wanted to stay and help people. Also, he didn't have a passport to get to Turkey.

Grandpa and Nana told us that it was a good idea that we come with them, but they had only one car for all of us and all their belongings. Grandpa wasn't sure that there would be enough space for all their children and grandchildren — eight people — in the car. He had a look on his face like he had a bad headache when he told us that, but he said we would figure it out.

I didn't know what I wanted. Was it better to fit or not fit? It was better for God to decide.

In the morning Uncle Saleh walked over and said that there was room for all of us, but we had to be ready to leave in thirty minutes. We had to pack fast — but we couldn't bring anything at all, not even any of my dolls. Mummy said we could get some clothes and pajamas in Turkey.

I was upset that I couldn't bring my dolls, but mainly I wanted to bring Baba.

There were so many people and so much stuff in the car; it was so tight that we were smushed together and couldn't move at all. So Baba couldn't have fit anyway, but I thought maybe we could find another car or throw away some things — something so that Baba could come with us. And we could explain to the people at the border why Baba didn't have a passport, and they would let us through because we are a family.

But Baba said, "No, Bana, I need to stay

79

here. I will see you soon." He picked me up, and he smelt like the cologne he always wore, like a mix of soap and trees, and thinking about how I wouldn't smell that anymore made me start to cry. I cried a lot this time. I couldn't help it.

"Don't cry, Bon Bon." But it's hard to make yourself stop crying even if you want to. Mohamed was crying too. Grandpa said that we had to go because the drive was going to be dangerous, and he wanted to leave before the planes came.

So we said good-bye. Baba kept waving, and I kept crying. I cried until I fell asleep, and when I woke up and it was almost nighttime and we were in Turkey.

ALL WE NEEDED WAS BABA.

I missed Baba. I had never spent a night away from him, except for the time that the *Mukhābarāt* took him away. We were staying in a house that we rented, but it wasn't like home, and it felt empty because Baba wasn't there. I was worried that something might happen to him while we were away. I got to talk to him every day, though. I always asked him when he was coming to visit. "Soon, Bana, soon," he would say. And then I would remind him to bring my dolls when he came. He promised he would.

A few weeks after we left, Grandpa and Grandma Alabed decided to leave Syria too — so Baba and his brothers had no parents nearby. Grandma and Grandpa went to a different town in Turkey that was a few hours' drive away from us. I was sad I didn't get to say good-bye to them, and I didn't know when I would see them again. I didn't like that everyone lived in a different place now. Family is all supposed to be together, not some here, some there.

Mummy found a nice doctor at a hospital in Turkey. He told Mummy scary news, though: the baby would be sick if it came now, so she had to take medicine to keep it inside so it could keep growing. We were all very worried, especially Mummy. She would run her hand over her belly and talk to the baby all the time. "You'll be okay. Please be okay," I could hear her whispering.

After two weeks the doctor said it was time for the baby to come. Mummy told me how the doctor was going to make a small hole in her stomach and pull the baby out, but it wouldn't hurt because they make it so you can't feel pain. That's how Mohamed and I had come too.

I couldn't be there when the doctor got the baby out because I wasn't allowed, but Nana and Grandpa took me to the hospital to see Mummy the next day. Mummy looked sick, but she was smiling. She was holding a blanket that looked like it was wrapped around a loaf of bread. But it wasn't bread — it was the baby.

Surprise: it was a boy. *Again.*

He was small and wrinkly. He looked like a baby chicken with no feathers. He smelled like fresh bread, though. Even though he

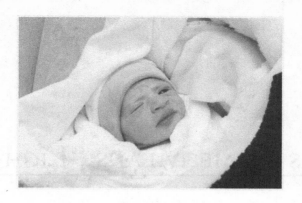

wasn't a girl, he did have blond hair, just like I had prayed for. I loved him when he was inside Mummy, but even more now that he was here.

We got to hold him for only a few minutes because he was small and weak, probably because of the war. Mummy said he was half the size I had been when I was born. At the hospital they put him under a lamp to keep him warm and help him grow.

Mummy was weak too. She looked tired and kind of gray. She did not have enough blood, so she had to stay in the hospital. We had to let her rest a lot, but I was allowed to spend a few hours with her every day. I would climb into the hospital bed with her and we would snuggle with the baby. All we needed was Baba.

His Name Means "Light."

I thought we would stay in Turkey for only a little while, but it was a long time because Mummy was sick and always tired. She needed Nana's help a lot, and she had to get stronger. I thought she would get stronger if she got to see Baba. She missed him as much as I did.

I told Mum that I missed Baba and my room and my desk and my books. I wanted to go home. Mummy said she missed home too. "We are homesick, Bana," she told me. That is when you feel sad because you're away from the place where you live and want to be.

After two months, Baba came to Turkey for a visit. It was dangerous because he had to get out of Aleppo and sneak across the border, since he didn't have a passport. When Baba came, so did Grandma and Grandpa Alabed from where they were in Turkey. Uncle Nezar came too. He had been

in the hospital in Turkey for a long time after a bomb hit his car while he was driving. All the glass in the windshield went into his face. It was a little scary to see him because he had no eyes or nose now. He couldn't see me anymore to see how big I had gotten since he saw me last, but I told him how tall I was.

Still, we were all so happy to see Baba and each other! You can't even imagine the feeling — like you are smiling so much your face hurts, and your body feels like it's full of butterflies, that's how happy you are. Even Nezar was excited; even though he couldn't actually see us anymore, he was happy we were all together and that he didn't have to be in the hospital anymore.

After getting all our hugs and kisses, Baba picked up the baby and smiled the biggest smile as he held him up to his face. With them side by side, you could tell they looked just alike.

"Nice to meet you, Noor," Baba said in a quiet voice.

That was what we called the baby: Noor.

His name means "light." Mummy said that's just what we needed.

It should have been the extreme exhaustion that tipped me off that I was pregnant. But I had been tired and on edge from the constant bombing for so long that I had long lost my ability to know what my body really felt like anymore. My wartime body was a run-down jangle of nerves and adrenaline.

And I had such a difficult time getting pregnant with both you and Mohamed, enduring so many treatments and surgeries, that it didn't even occur to me that it would be possible that I could become pregnant again. Besides, I was trying hard enough to keep the children I already had alive; it was breathtakingly absurd to think of bringing a baby into the equation. And yet it was so. I was pregnant.

The war in Aleppo had been raging for almost a year at this point, and we were consumed by fear and uncertainty. So rather than this being the happiest news, like it was with you and Mohamed, I was devastated and overcome with cold fear and dread.

How would we feed this baby? How and where would I deliver, given that I couldn't go to the hospital in West Aleppo where you were born, and many of the hospitals in East Aleppo had been destroyed, including the one where Mohamed was born? And my previous two pregnancies had been difficult, as had both births and my recovery afterward. How would I manage without medical care?

Even if somehow I was able to have a safe and healthy birth, how would we raise this baby? There were so few resources and so little safe water. Already there were reports of babies being born with birth defects because of all the chemicals from the bombings, or babies who were premature and sick because of lack of food and because the pervasive fear and stress affected their mother's bodies.

It was madness to bring a life into a world plagued by so much death. It was unthinkable.

Your baba and I agonized about what we would do. In our desperation and our darkest hour, it crossed our minds to try to find some way to end the pregnancy. It was horrible to even contemplate, but that was how desperate we were. We reached out to my friend Asma, who was a nurse, to find someone to help us. But in the end, I just couldn't go through with it.

The truth was, the fact that I was pregnant was a miracle, and I wanted another child. War aside, that was the simple fact of it. And I could picture this little boy — somehow I knew it was a boy — just like I had been able to clearly picture you, Bana.

I was already his mother, even though he wasn't here yet. The war had robbed us of so much that I couldn't — I wouldn't — let it take away our baby. Even understanding that there would likely be the constant threat of death from that moment on, I believed he deserved a chance to live.

And so it was decided. Though I can't say I felt fully happy about it until I told you. Do you remember? You clapped and squealed. "A baby for me?" you said. "Well, for all of us," I explained.

It was then that I allowed myself just a bit of happiness and excitement. Sharing in your joy allowed me to finally tap into my own and to put aside — at least for the moment — all the fear and anxiety.

When I was pregnant with you and Mohamed, I had so many checkups all the time, and it was a comfort to know that you were growing little fingers and toes and lungs and that you were healthy. With Noor, I had no good access to medical care, and that was terrifying. Since Asma was a nurse, she sometimes had access to an ultrasound, and twice she gave me one. You came with me, and you were so amazed that you could see the baby on the screen and hear his heartbeat. You carried the ultrasound picture everywhere you went and showed everybody in the family. "Look, that's the baby inside Mummy!" you would say, full of wonder.

You had so many plans and dreams for the baby — first that he would be blond. I thought that was a long shot, since all the rest of us have dark hair, but sure enough, you got your wish.

Sometimes when the bombings raged on we would sit in the basement and you would tell me everything you would teach him and show him. It made for a strange time: here we were cowering like rabbits as bombs rained down, unsure of what the night or the next day would bring, and you were singing songs and spinning tales of a future brighter than any firebomb.

Even as we listened to your big dreams, the primal goal we had at the moment was much more urgent: keep everyone alive. That is the nature of war — planning for the future with the exact same resolve and urgency as preparing for the possibility that you might not have one.

The last few months of my pregnancy came during a relatively calm time in Aleppo — it was almost as though I had wished it so with my urgent prayers that the baby would enter the world in peace. But in a cruel and terrible twist, the weeks before my due date brought a period of intense bombing. It was as if the war were mocking me.

One night, I was haunted by a particularly ominous feeling that I would die in childbirth if I had to deliver in our apartment, which was still a better option than the hospitals, since they were barely operating and were always targets.

That same night was one of the most relentless bombings we'd had in months. I was terrified that I would go into labor in the basement. Usually we tried to read and sing, but this night I couldn't do more than pray and take short, shallow breaths and try to block out the pain and the panic.

The next morning, when there was a lull, we went upstairs, skittish and shaking in the thin gray light.

Given how close the bombs had been, we dreaded surveying the damage — a demoralizing ritual. We quickly learned that Nana and Grandpa's house was destroyed and that Abdo had been gravely injured. For my parents, who were already ready to leave, this was the final straw. They were out of options and exhausted from feeling like sitting ducks. I understood their desire to leave, but still lamented. What was home without my parents? I was a grown-up; twenty-five years old with a husband and two kids, and one more on the way, but you always need your mum, Bana.

They decided to leave the next day and go to Urfa, a town in Turkey right on the border with Syria. Ghassan and I talked and agonized over our options and decided that I should go with my parents if I could. I couldn't have this baby in Syria — I remained consumed by the feeling that the baby would die or I would, or both. But the thought of leaving your father behind and being without him in Turkey made me feel sick with fear and loneliness. Ghassan, after all, was my rock and my source of strength. Your father is an amazing man — strong and steadfast. I couldn't imagine ever being without him.

So again, we weighed two evils: stay or go. In the end, my gut told me I had to go — I had no choice. And to this day, I believe in my heart of hearts that I would have died if I had stayed. Given how sick I was after giving birth and how much blood I lost, if I hadn't had the medical care I did, the story would have ended quite differently. Still, leaving Syria and Baba that day was one of the hardest things I have ever done.

And do you remember how you cried, Bana? I had never seen you cry like that. You didn't want me to leave you, and how could I? But you didn't want to leave Baba either. Splitting up our family was excruciating for us all. It was hours into the drive before you calmed down and fell into an exhausted sleep in my lap. I was so happy to have you with me, little one. You gave me strength — which I had never needed more in my life. Giving birth in a strange country without your father by my side was one of the loneliest experiences of my life. But then the baby was here, healthy but so much smaller than you and Mohamed had been. He looked exactly like the fair-skinned little boy you had pictured, with an improbable tuft of silky blond hair. As I felt his warmth on my chest for the first time, everything else faded away: the bombs, the loss, the despair, the fear that had become a part of me. In their place came a sense of calm I hadn't experienced in years. The world receded to nothing but his heartbeat against mine, a steadying and nourishing force.

In that moment, I felt . . . fortified, invincible. I had brought beauty and life into the world, and that force is infinitely more powerful than guns and bombs and evil. It is the most simple calculation in the universe: life is the antidote to death, as light is the antidote to darkness.

Your baby brother was a light in the darkness, so we named him Noor. His birth felt like a sign that the world could — that it would — get better, and it gave me hope that, despite the odds, my country would be able to sustain the fragility of his life, that his birth would be a testament to and an omen for a renewed humanity, and just as his life was a fresh start, so might we have one in Aleppo. And so it seemed for a while that this would be so. Baba told us how much better things now were in Syria. For months it had been calmer; life seemed to be going back to normal. Baba had found a new job. So after five long months of being away, I was feeling stronger, and it was time to go home. We believed we were returning to a brighter new day.

Oh, Bana, how wrong we were.

When You're Homesick, You Feel Better When You Go Home.

We decided to go back to Syria. Baba told us that things had been better in Aleppo — lately there were fewer bombs. He even went back to work. He said we should come home, which was happy news for Mummy and me.

But Nana and Grandpa were not happy when we told them we were going to go back to Aleppo. There were angry voices. Grandpa said, "This is madness, Fatemah. You have the baby now. You're safe here. It is suicide to return."

Mummy said that Baba had a job again, and if he came to Turkey, he wouldn't have any work. She reminded them that things were much better, and promised that if things got bad again, we would pack up the house and come right back. But we had to go back to Aleppo — if only to get all our belongings. We couldn't just leave everything behind.

I agreed, because I needed to get my dolls, my books, the pictures I had drawn, and everything else. Also, I didn't get to say good-bye to Yasmin and my other friends before we came to Turkey. I didn't want to say good-bye to them, though. I told Grandpa I wanted to go home to Syria for good.

He let out a big sigh. "I know, Bana," he said. "But we want you to stay here and be safe."

A small part of me wanted to stay too, because I was a little bit nervous to go back to Aleppo because the bombs could come back. But mostly I was excited, because when you're homesick, you feel better when you go home.

And so we did.

I Didn't Want My Little Brother to Ever Have to Feel Afraid.

Baba was right: it was much better. It was almost like the war was over and life was normal again — though I sometimes forgot what regular life was anymore, it had been so long. Noor got bigger and started crawling and then walking, and there were barely any bombs. It was nearly like when I was a baby. There were still reminders, though. They didn't fix all the crumbled buildings, and the water and electricity still came on only two or three times a week, but I didn't feel so scared all the time, and that was nice. I thought that maybe Noor would be lucky — maybe he would never have to know the bombs and bullets and fighting. I didn't want my little brother to ever have to feel afraid. He was just a baby.

Also, if the war stayed away, maybe Noor could learn to swim like me, though Alrabea Pool had been destroyed by a bomb. They would have to build another one. Or, when Noor got bigger, we could take him to the market to get Jell-O. There were still a lot of stores that were closed, though. And the stores that were open didn't have what you wanted a lot of the time.

Once we got to take Noor on a Ferris wheel. It was my favorite holiday, Eid. We all went to the market to try to buy some special treats for the holiday. There was a man in our neighborhood who had a little cart that could make cotton candy, so we got some. Our lips and tongues turned pink. One time, I brought the man some sugar from our house, because it was hard to get sugar sometimes with the war. I told him he could have it so he could make more cotton candy for other kids.

Some other families were out walking too, and everyone smiled at one another a lot because we were all so happy. Mummy said that everyone was healing and feeling better, so we were all in good moods. A little Ferris wheel had been set up in the park near our house, and we went for a ride. Baba said we could ride for only a few minutes because he was still nervous about being outside for a long time. It's hard for that feeling to go away, even when you are safe.

Noor didn't love the Ferris wheel like I

thought he would — he cried at the top the first time around, but then he got used to it and liked it more. We went round and round for ten minutes. Mummy and Baba watched us and smiled and waved and took our picture. When you go through so many bad things, you notice the nice times more and feel even happier for them. That day, we were so happy that it was almost like we forgot there was ever war at all.

Maybe We Could Learn How to Stop the War.

The best thing about when the war got better was school. Mummy and some of her friends got together and decided to make a school for all the children in our neighborhood. There were no schools in East Aleppo anymore because the regime had bombed them all. So many kids died right at their desks while they were just trying to learn. Mummy felt bad that we children had no place to learn and nothing to do during the day. Mummy always talks about how important education is and how all children should be in school so they can learn to help people when they grow up, so we can have doctors and teachers and lawyers like Baba to make Syria strong. Maybe we could learn how to stop the war.

Mummy and her friends asked neighbors for paper and books and whatever they could share. There were also some people in our neighborhood who got together to

101

help people, and they helped us find school supplies.

School was down the street from our house in the basement of an apartment building that was now empty because everyone had moved away. Mummy said our school must be kept a secret so it wouldn't be bombed.

There were only about one hundred children every day. There could have been more, but some parents were still scared to send their children outside, even though the bombs were better. Like I said, it's hard to stop being scared. Also, a lot of people were gone — they had moved away or been killed.

We sat on the floor in the basement, which was a little dusty and dark, just like our basement at home, but I didn't mind because it was school. There were three sections: one with little children like Mohamed and Noor; one with bigger children like me; and then one with older children. My mum taught some of the older children who were learning about math and how to write well. My teacher was Farah, and she taught us many interesting things like how eggs become chickens, how to write our names in Arabic and English, and what our different body parts do. We did this three days per week, and these were the best three days of

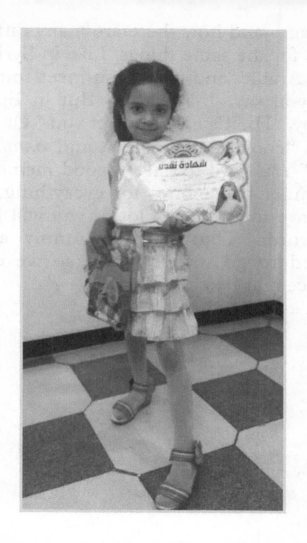

the week.

Mummy also went to school for three days like me. It wasn't the same as her university classes, but she and her friends had a school where they learned and practiced their English. At home, Mummy would teach me English too. It's fun to learn different languages and how there are many different words for the same things. Like in Syria, we speak Arabic, and when you meet someone new, you say, "Marhaba." But in English you say, "Hi, it's nice to meet you." Or *baskwyt* is "cookie" in English, and *dammia* is "doll." You have to have a good memory to remember two names for everything. And you have to practice a lot or you will forget the words. That's why Mummy and I wanted to go to school — so we could practice and be clever.

"How Was Your Day, Little One?"

When there was school for Mummy and me and Baba went back to work, it was almost like the old days, except Noor and Mohamed and I couldn't stay at Nana Samar's, since she lived in Turkey now. I was big now, though, so I could help watch Noor and Mohamed when Mummy and Baba weren't home. I would have school for my brothers at home and teach them. I was trying to teach Noor how to talk, but he couldn't say any words yet. Mummy said he didn't talk because he was scared from the bombs, even if there weren't as many as before. Sometimes when you are scared all the time your body and brain do different things, even if you don't mean for them to — like stop talking or wet yourself or have bad dreams or shake a lot. All of that would happen to us.

I was teaching Mohamed about colors and counting, but sometimes he didn't listen

and just wanted to play with trucks, which was annoying. Sometimes, even though I wasn't supposed to, I would take them to the roof of our apartment building, where we had a garden. But up there it was big, so we could run back and forth, back and forth, and spin around until we were dizzy, and we all loved to do that. Sometimes Yasmin would come over and we would take our jump ropes to the roof and practice.

One day, I decided on a surprise. I was going to take Noor and Mohamed to go visit Baba. His office was just down the street. We weren't allowed to leave the house, but I thought Baba would like the surprise and wouldn't be mad. When we got outside, I could tell that my brothers were a little nervous. It was a good day — only one or two bombs so far, and very far away — so I told them not to worry. But after we had been walking for a while, there was a rumble in the sky, and Noor got scared and wet himself. And then he started to cry a lot. I told him it was okay, but we couldn't go to Baba's like that. So I had to take him home and give him a bath. I washed out his pants in the sink so Mummy wouldn't find out. When she got home she asked, "How was your day, little one?" I didn't tell her about the surprise.

HOPE IS WHEN YOU FEEL LIKE THE WORLD IS BEAUTIFUL.

When the war went away, we had hope. Hope is when you feel like the world is beautiful and that you can do anything. You feel like you can get through anything bad that happens, because it will be good again soon. So if you have hope, you can still be a little bit happy even if things you don't like are happening, because you know it will get better. When you don't have hope, it's like you are waiting for bad things to happen to you or you think it will always be bad, and that actually makes everything feel even worse. So you should always try to have hope.

But it also can be hard when you believe that good things will happen and they don't. I had hope that the bombs were gone for good. But they weren't. Even though I hoped so hard that the war would be over, it didn't work. Instead, everything became worse than ever.

"Just Bombs, Bombs, Bombs."

Like someone pressed a button, all the big bombs started falling again, and every day was a very bad day all over again. The planes filled the skies all the time and dropped bomb after bomb. It was never quiet anymore. I forgot what quiet even sounded like.

Mummy and I still wanted to have school, but every time we went there were fewer and fewer children because people were too scared to go outside.

One day there were just fifteen or so children, and we were all studying and learning when we heard the warplanes in the air in the distance. Mummy and Farah decided that we should all go home — it was too dangerous. I was sad that school was over early, but Mummy said we could keep practicing at home.

We walked home quickly, because a bomb could drop at any moment. When the planes came, you only had time to count to three,

maybe to five, and then **BOOM**, so if you were outside, there wasn't much time to run and hide. Before we got to our house there was a huge boom — the louder the boom, the closer the bomb. This was really close. We ran the rest of the way so we could get to the basement.

Mummy's phone started to ring. It was Baba. I could hear him through the phone because he was yelling: *"Where are you? Are you okay? Did you hear what happened?"* He didn't even let her answer between questions.

"We're okay, Ghassan. We're at home. What happened?"

"Oh, thank God," Baba said. "They bombed the school!" He was at the market and could see the huge cloud of smoke. Everyone started telling him that the school was bombed and they had to run and help the kids. But we had all left.

Baba kept saying thanks to Allah over and over again that we were alive. But I felt sad. It's not as sad as a person dying, but still, I would miss my school. Now I wouldn't get to go anymore. I could tell everything was going to be like it was before. No school, no work, no shopping, no going outside — just bombs, bombs, bombs.

WHAT DOES IT FEEL LIKE TO DIE?

Then there was a very awful day I wish I could forget.

I woke up because there was a rumble like an earthquake and then a loud crashing. The sound and shaking were so loud they felt like they could break my bones. When the bombs fall right on top of you like this, you can't hear anything. It's like all the noise in the world at once, but at the same time it's like someone is holding a pillow on your head. Everything shakes so you feel it in your bones and your insides — even in your teeth. And it's like the air is pressing down on you, trying to smash you into the ground.

I started screaming for Mummy.

It looked like night outside, even though it was early morning. There was so much dust in the air. I could see a bright light out the window through all the smoke — the building across the street was on fire. I was looking out the window where our balcony was — or where it used to be, because it had been blown off, and glass from the balcony door was everywhere.

Baba scooped up Noor and Mohamed, and Mummy grabbed my hand and we all ran for the basement as fast as we could. The front door to our apartment was blown off and just hanging there.

Even in the basement we could still feel the shaking and hear the booms. We were all quiet and praying to ourselves. We said *"Ya lateef"* over and over whenever we were in the basement. We were asking God to have mercy on us.

I was so afraid that our building would collapse on top of us and leave us buried under all the rocks. I kept wondering what it would feel like. What does it feel like to die?

When it seemed like the bombs had stopped, Baba said he would go up first alone and look to see if things were safe. After a few minutes he called to us and said we could come up, but his voice sounded funny.

When we got upstairs, it was very, very bad. It looked like someone had taken a hammer to our street and crushed it into a million pieces. I couldn't believe it, but the building next door was completely crushed up like it had never even been there. Part of it had fallen onto our building and smashed the floor above us, where Uncle Mazen lived. Our balcony had fallen down onto our car and buried it so that we could barely even see it. I guess we didn't need a car anymore, since there were not many roads to drive on or anywhere to go.

You could hear many people screaming and crying. Whenever there was a bomb like this, all the neighbors called out to each other to try to figure out who was missing. They called for Baba: "Ghassan, is your family okay?"

"We are all okay!" Baba called back. And then all the families who are okay go to help everyone else. If people are hurt or buried under the rubble, you have to move fast to get them out.

One person's screams were louder than everyone else's. It was Yasmin's mum yelling, "No, no, no, no!" I got a funny feeling in my stomach. Yasmin and her mum lived in the building that wasn't there anymore.

Mummy and I ran over with the other neighbors. Yasmin's mum's black hair was completely white with dust like she were old. The only place she didn't have dust was on her cheeks, where tears were running

115

down her face.

Other volunteers arrived to help us. Since we didn't have any more ambulances or police to help us in East Aleppo, there was a group of people who volunteered to help when people were hurt or trapped in the rubble after bombings. Or they tried to fix people if they were cut or had broken parts. It was very dangerous for them, because the regime didn't like anyone who was helping people. So when the volunteers arrived after a bomb, the warplanes would sometimes come back again just to bomb them too.

They were all hurrying and digging and calling to one another as they pulled bodies out. Then one of the men lifted a body out of the rocks, and there was more screaming from Yasmin's mum. It was Yasmin. She was floppy like she was asleep, and had a lot of blood and dust on her. I couldn't move or breathe because I was so scared seeing my friend like that. They took her away in a truck they had turned into an ambulance. I prayed so much that she would be okay. Mum hugged me tight and said, "Come on, Bon Bon, let's go home." I couldn't play the rest of the day — all I could do was see Yasmin and all the blood on her in my mind.

Later that night, when we were still trying to clean up our apartment from the bomb-

ing, we heard lots of crying and praying outside. Our street was filled with people who were taking bodies to the mosque to have prayers for them. This happened every time there was a big bombing. They used to bury people in the cemetery after the prayers, but with the war, all the cemeteries became full, so they put dead people in the ground in the parks.

I had asked Mummy many times that day if Yasmin was okay. Mummy said they had taken her to the doctor and that we would have to pray a lot. That night I heard and saw Yasmin's mummy crying in the street.

The next day I saw her on the street again, and she was still crying a lot.

"Yasmin isn't here anymore, Bana," she said. I knew what she meant. Yasmin was dead.

I Wouldn't Get to Play with Her Ever Again.

After Yasmin was gone, I was even more scared to die. I couldn't stop thinking about what it would feel like.

I was also scared for my brothers or my parents to die. Sometimes I thought about what would be the worst thing. If Mummy died? Or Baba? Or my brothers? If we all died together, that would be the best. Then no one would have to miss anyone.

Mummy says that if you are good and kind, God will love you and protect you and that you get to go to Heaven when you die. In Heaven, there are lots of sweets and games — it is a good place, and you get to stay there forever. I hope that Yasmin is happy there.

But I missed my friend very much. It's different to miss someone who is still alive than it is to miss one who is dead. I missed my grandparents and uncles who moved away, but they were still alive, and it made me miss them less when we talked on Whats-App and the phone. But the way I missed Yasmin was different. It gave me a feeling like I was sinking inside. I couldn't talk to her. We wouldn't get to dress up in our favorite princess dresses ever again. I bet Yasmin's favorite dresses were all under the rubble still.

When it was time for my birthday, I wasn't feeling excited like I normally am for a birthday. It was a month after Yasmin died, and she couldn't come over to celebrate that was I seven now. She had always come to my birthdays before.

Mummy and Baba tried to make a celebration, even though it was too dangerous for anyone to come over and there were bombs all night so we had to stay in the basement. There wasn't much food at the markets, so I didn't get to have a cake. But we still got to be together as a family, and that is always nice. Uncle Wesam gave me a pretty new doll. It was my favorite as soon as I saw it. She had a pink hat and pink boots, just like the ones I got for Eid last year. I usually didn't name my dolls, but this one I did. I decided to call her Yasmin.

I also got another special present: an iPad of my very own. It had been used by someone else before, but that was okay. Baba had

to go to a lot of trouble to get this special treat in the war, because the stores didn't have many new things. But he wanted to do something extra nice, since it was my birthday. I could watch TV and read on my new iPad, which was good, because we didn't get to go outside much anymore. I would always use Mummy's phone so that I could talk to my uncles and cousins on WhatsApp because I missed them so much.

Now I could talk to them on my iPad. I could watch my favorite cartoons and read books and try to forget about the bad feelings. Sometimes it worked, and sometimes it didn't.

I didn't get to have birthday candles to blow out and make a wish on, but I still made one anyway: that no one else would die.

It is a miracle that you are alive, Bana. I believe that with all my heart. That all three of my children and my husband survived six years of war fills me with more than just overwhelming gratitude, it fills me with awe. It doesn't seem possible — or fair — that we should be so fortunate. It is strange to think of all we've been through and all that we have lost and still consider ourselves so fortunate, but we are. And I feel the luckiest of all because all my children are alive and now safe. For so many thousands of other mothers, that is not the case.

One of the worst parts of war is how easily you can become accustomed to the violence and death around you. For many long stretches, when hundreds of people were dying in Aleppo every day, it was a constant grim ritual to receive news of someone — a friend, a neighbor, a cousin — who had died in the bombings. Learning of death — not to mention accepting it as a daily prospect — became a morbid routine, and the only way you could keep going was to settle into a certain numbness to whatever extent was possible.

It was a blessing and a curse to harden to the horrors. But sometimes as inured as you hoped to be to the onslaught of heartbreak, something would happen to shatter that protective wall and pierce you through and through. That was the case when Yasmin died. You two were so close, like family. The look on Yasmin's mother's face that day will stay with me forever. You don't know true pain until you've looked into the eyes of a mother who has lost her child. It's almost as if her grief were physical, as if the despair were a heavy stone loosed from the rubble and placed on her back, crushing her with its weight. I wish it were something physical like that, actually, because at least I could have helped her carry that burden; I could have lifted that rock. But there was so little I could do to make anything better for her. I knew exactly what she was thinking that day while they dug Yasmin out of the rubble, because it was exactly what I would have been thinking: I wish it had been me. And also: How will I go on? And yet somehow we do.

There is another story that haunts me, about the woman who lived down the street from us, who I knew through Asma. One night she put her four kids to bed, just like I would put you three. Like you and your brothers, her little ones were also scared to sleep alone during the war, so she put them all in bed together in the safest place she knew, on a mattress in the middle of her home, away from the windows. But when a bomb hit the building next door, the aftershocks were so strong that one wall of her apartment fell in, crashing down right on top of her sleeping babies. In an instant, all of her children were gone. This happened, and yet it is still unimaginable. Of all the agonizing stories, it is hers that haunts me, that gives me nightmares to this day. I dream I am looking down on the mangled bodies of my crushed children, trying desperately to unearth you from under a mountain of rubble. I wake up in a cold sweat and rush to your room. The three of you still insist on sharing one bed, coiled against one another like a litter of puppies. I'll stand there and watch you sleep, matching my breaths to yours, until my heart rate returns to normal. And then I pray for this mother, that wherever she is, she has found peace or something close to it, a way to go on.

When I think of her and Yasmin's mother and all the people who have died in our homeland over the last six years and counting

— hundreds of thousands of our friends and neighbors and fellow Syrians — it's unbearable. So many mothers, sisters, sons, children — so many children — all gone. And when I think of the suffering and brutality of the deaths — like those children who died in particular agony because of chemical bombs — I wonder, how could we let that happen?

And every day, there are still more deaths: people dying in the violence, or dying of malnutrition and illness in camps, or dying as they try in desperation to escape by crossing the desert or the sea. Like the little boy Alan Kurdi, made famous when the photo of his body on the beach was shared globally. He was the exact same age as Noor; that could have been Noor. All these deaths, all this misery, and so meaningless.

I tell your father how guilty I feel that we should be so fortunate, that we have been spared. We did nothing to deserve to live, and our fellow Syrians did nothing to deserve to die. And the cruelty of that scenario can undo me if I allow it.

Oh, Bana, having to explain death to you was one of my hardest tasks as a mother. Before the war you hadn't known death yet, and then suddenly it was all around you. When Yasmin died, I could see the fear and sadness in your eyes, and there was nothing I could do to take the pain from you. Something inside you changed that day — it was the final loss of innocence. It was the last day of your childhood.

There are no children in Syria. You all were forced to become adults — to understand killing, to experience fear and starvation and pain in a way that all children should be shielded from. But that was a luxury we did not have.

Something changed for me too when Yasmin died, and when the siege overtook us in those brutal months after. Along with being terrified and heartbroken, I became angry — angry that we had to endure this while the world did nothing. Angry that I was helpless to protect my children. Angry that there is a world where bombing and killing children is tolerated. Angry that I taught you to be generous and fair and kind and then offered you a world that was anything but.

As things became more desperate so too did your questions: Do people know this is happening to us? Does anyone care? Why do they keep bombing us? Why won't they stop? Why can't we have peace?

I was angry most of all that I didn't have answers to those questions.

And that you, a seven-year-old girl, had to ask them.

"I Can't Believe They Could Be This Cruel."

Now it was Ramadan, and the warplanes came on purpose right as the sun went down, when it was time for *iftar,* which is when you break the fast and have a big meal with your family after not eating all day. The planes bombed us right then so that people couldn't make any food to eat or go to mosque for Ramadan prayers. This was extra mean. Grandma Alabed said, "I can't believe they could be this cruel."

She and Grandpa Alabed were back from Turkey. They came to visit for a few months when things had been better because they missed Baba and their other children and us grandchildren so much. But when it got bad again they got stuck, because it was harder to leave Syria. Grandma Alabed was always in the wrong place.

One night when Ramadan was almost over, Mummy and Baba and the rest of the family were talking a lot in serious voices.

Everyone in East Aleppo was saying that the regime's army was going to surround us and try to get the Free Syrian Army to give up once and for all. They would make it so that no one would be allowed to come into East Aleppo at all, to bring medicine or food or clothes or anything. No one would be allowed out either. We would be trapped. It is *hisar.* A siege.

Baba and Mummy said we had to get ready for this — and fast. We would need to get as much as we could of the things we needed so we wouldn't run out. We had to do this quickly, before the stores ran out. Baba went out early the next morning and bought supplies — lots of medicines at the pharmacy and big sacks of food that wouldn't go bad and that you could make with just water, like rice and macaroni and dry soup. I already missed eating chips and pizza. But Mummy said we were lucky, because so many people couldn't afford to have any food to eat at all because the war made it expensive. I wondered what would happen when we ate all of our food if there was no way to get more. We had to be careful and eat only a little at a time, even if we were hungry.

Baba also got as much fuel as he could so we could work our generator. We used the generator to pump water up from the well. We made sure we had plenty of water in a big container on the roof. Baba and my uncles went to fill it up in the middle of the night when the bombs stopped, because during the day the regime sent planes to take pictures of everyone's houses, and Baba didn't want the army to take a picture of him on the roof.

We had our solar panels so we could charge our phones and my iPad and run our lights, so that was good. The war would have been much worse if I hadn't had my iPad.

We got everything we could to be ready, which was good because at the end of Ramadan, two days after Eid al-Fitr, the government army circled tanks all around East Aleppo. The siege was here.

WE TOOK TURNS HELPING EACH OTHER HAVE HOPE.

We didn't know if the siege would ever end, and that was scary. If we never got to have food or medicine again, then we would just starve or get sick and die. That's what the regime wanted. But the Free Syrian Army was fighting all around East Aleppo to make a hole so people and things could come and go from that part of the city.

All day and all night we heard the fighting. Yelling and guns, and helicopters and planes. War is very loud. I always had a headache.

There was nothing we could do but wait and hope and eat only macaroni and rice. We took baths just once a week so that we could save water.

Four times a week we could get bread from the Local Council of East Aleppo. This was a group that volunteered to help people in East Aleppo after we were cut off from West Aleppo. Baba worked there sometimes.

131

They had a list of all the families in each neighborhood, and you could go get one piece of bread per person. Once the regime realized that people were lining up to get bread, though, they started bombing the bread lines. So the council moved around and the neighbors kept it a secret where the bread would be next so the regime didn't know ahead of time.

We all tried to help each other like this in East Aleppo. We shared whatever we could — like we would all share generators and each take turns having some power so that we could charge phones or watch TV or have some lights. Or if someone got hurt, we would share bandages and any medicine we had.

We helped each other in my family too. I liked that my aunts and uncles and cousins lived in one building and we could all be together. Sometimes Baba would help Uncle Wesam feel better, and Aunt Fatemah would make my mum feel better, like I would make Noor feel better. We took turns helping each other have hope.

I Prayed That the Plan Would Work.

After three weeks of the siege, the Free Syrian Army made a plan to fight back, and everyone helped. One night the air filled with the worst smell ever — it was burning rubber, and it made your nose sting. People had set tires on fire in the street. The plan was that we would make a big cloud of thick smoke over East Aleppo so the warplanes couldn't see us and wouldn't be able to drop any bombs, and then the Free Syrian Army could go make a hole to break the siege. It was a clever idea to hide like this, but it also made the air so smoky and smelly that my eyes would water all the time.

Everyone started burning things in the streets — first tires, and then garbage and whatever they could find. I wanted to go help, but Mummy said I wasn't allowed and could only watch from the window. We had only a few families left on our street — everyone else had left or been killed — but

there were a lot of people out, more than
since the bombs started. I prayed that the
plan would work.

I could never get used to the awful smell,
though — even after one day, and two days,
and three days. The air smelt worse and
worse, and the smoke made us cough.
Everything was black and gray. But that was
okay, because the plan worked! After one
week of fighting, the Free Syrian Army
broke through where the army was, and the
siege was broken. We did it!

Everybody in East Aleppo was so happy
and so proud — people ran into the streets
and were hugging and cheering. Through
all of East Aleppo you could hear the sound
of Eid prayers ringing out from the

mosques. Even though it wasn't Eid, all the mosques played the special prayers from the speakers that send out the call to prayer so it would give people courage.

We were excited, because the Free Syrian Army had a big victory and it could be different now. Our hope and prayers finally worked. Maybe now they could get the regime to stop bombing us and the war would be over.

The next day, everyone got even more happy when trucks arrived with food and supplies. We all went to get some so there were lines, but no one cared. Eggs! Chicken! Tomatoes! We were scared we would never see this food again. People were laughing and planning what they would make for dinner. Mohamed, Noor, and I all jumped up and down when we saw the food that Baba brought home, like apples and cucumbers and watermelons. They were so beautiful. Mummy said she would make us a special dinner — fried chicken. She also made us hard-boiled eggs. Mohamed, Noor, and I were so excited to have eggs that we ate a dozen! I'm glad we could have such a feast, because it was the last time I would get to have any eggs, milk, fruit, or meat in Aleppo.

You Can Almost Feel Like It's Real.

The regime's army was very strong. In just ten days, the siege was back again — and I think the regime was mad that the Free Syrian Army broke through, because they bombed us even more, and the fights between the armies were louder, closer. So we were scared all over again. Especially Noor. Every time there was a loud noise he would freeze like a statue and then start to cry. He still couldn't say any words — he could only cry, which he did a lot.

One time, instead of freezing when he heard the rumble of the warplanes, he got so scared that he ran into a wall and cut his head open. There was so much blood. Mummy said he needed a hospital, but it was dangerous to go to the hospitals, since they got bombed all the time. We would fix them as much as we could, and the regime would bomb them again, and on and on. So we didn't know what to do. Uncles Mazen

and Yaman said they would take him.

I was hugging Noor tight even though I got blood on me. I was scared for him to go to the hospital in case it got bombed while he was there. Mummy said I had to let go of him and let my uncles take him, but she was very upset too.

We had to wait for almost two hours for him to come home, but he was okay. He just needed two stitches. I sat with him in my lap and read books to him to try to make him feel better.

I always tried to take care of Noor and Mohamed and my little cousins as much as I could, because I'm the oldest. It was my job to distract them from feeling sad or scared. When my iPad was charged (sometimes it went dead if we didn't have enough power from the solar panels), I let Mohamed watch as much *SpongeBob SquarePants* as he wanted. Or sometimes I would hug my brothers and hold them — especially when the bombs were bad and they were frightened — and tell them, "It's going to be okay."

Sometimes I would tell them stories, like the one about the wolf trying to trick the baby sheep. Or I would tell them about what life was going to be like when the war was finally over: We would eat as many sweets as we wanted. And we would get to see Nana Samar and Grandpa Malek again. And they would fix all the schools and parks, and we could play outside. I told them how to imagine it — to think about it with your mind like it's a dream while you're awake, and you can almost feel like it's real.

One time after we hadn't been able to go outside in a long time because of the siege, I had the best idea to cheer us up! First, I hooked my jump rope in a doorway to make a swing. Then I pulled the mattress off my

bed and put it up against the frame so we could slide on it. And I took long pieces of wood from the pile that we were burning to keep warm, since there was little fuel, and put them over a big pile of pillows to make a seesaw. It was just like a real seesaw! We now had a whole playground inside. Even if it wasn't as good as getting to go to a real park, it was fun.

Mummy loved my playground and told me how clever I was. She had good ideas too — like if we ever had any extra water, she would blow up our plastic swimming pool, and we could swim in the living room. Or after she cleaned the floors, we could use any extra water to slide across them like a waterslide.

We had to be extra clever like that in making up games, since we couldn't do the things other kids get to do because they don't have war — like go to a pool to swim and go on real swings and play football outside. I tried to do things that were fun, like playing in the inside playground or reading good books or writing or making up songs and games to cheer up my brothers and cousins. We had to play, or it just felt like all we did was wait for the bombs to see who died.

EVERY DAY THERE WAS LESS AND LESS OF EVERYTHING.

The Free Syrian Army didn't have another plan, so the siege went on and on. By the time it was Eid al-Adha, there was no food in the market for a feast or clothes in the stores to get new clothes like you're supposed to. And everything was dirty and dusty from all the bombs, so it was hard to make the house sparkling clean. Usually Eid al-Fitr and Eid al-Adha are the two best days of the year, but this time the holiday wasn't very fun since we couldn't celebrate, and that made everyone feel sad. I didn't know if it was my favorite holiday anymore.

I needed new clothes, since I was growing and it was getting cold, but there were no clothes for girls in the stores anymore. I had to get boys' clothes, and it made me upset. I like dresses and pink and all girls' clothes. Mummy said, "This is the best we can do, Bana. I'm sorry." I didn't want her to feel bad so I tried to stop crying, but I hated

those boy clothes.

Every day there was less and less of everything. There was little medicine for people at the hospital, and no more fuel for cars or generators, so they couldn't run anymore. There wasn't even any more flour so that people could make bread. We were lucky that we had saved so much food and fuel, even though I hated to eat macaroni and rice over and over and over again. I knew some children didn't have any food at all.

Baba took me to get seeds and we made a little garden on the roof to try to grow vegetables, since we couldn't get them anymore. Aunt Zena gave us the idea. When the first siege started, people planted seeds. She and the people in her building shared a few tomato plants. We didn't get to visit her much anymore because it wasn't safe to walk outside, but one day when there weren't as many bombs Mummy and I went over, and Aunt Zena had saved a tomato for us. I was so happy to see it — it was like it glowed when it came out of her pocket. I hadn't seen a tomato in a long time. I was so hungry that I wanted to bite into that juicy tomato right then, but I tucked it into my pocket so I could share it with Mohamed and Noor. When we got home, I cut the tomato in five equal parts, one for each of us. I don't know what was better: the tomato, or how happy we all were to share, even if it was only one bite.

MAYBE SOMEONE WOULD DO SOMETHING BEFORE IT WAS TOO LATE.

I was so sick of the siege and the bombs. To be scared all the time and to see people getting hurt and dying while also trying to have hope makes you so tired. I didn't think life would ever go back to happy times like before; it was only getting worse.

I asked Mummy if people outside Syria and Aleppo knew what was happening to us. Why didn't anyone tell the regime to stop killing people? You're supposed to be kind and help people. This is what Baba and Mummy taught us.

So there is no good reason for war. It is not right for so many people and children to die. Because after everyone is dead, then what? What will be different?

There used to be a lot of people in Aleppo and in my country, but many left and many have died. So I don't know who will fix all the broken buildings or build new schools. Who will be able to live there?

It's like when I lost some pieces to my favorite puzzle. I couldn't get new pieces, so I couldn't put it back together again anymore. I could only throw it away and get a new puzzle, but we can't get a new Syria.

We were feeling that we would never be able to leave Aleppo and would just have to wait until a bomb fell on us and we all died. I wanted to do something, so I wrote a message on Twitter: "I need peace."

By the time I wrote this message, we had been in the second siege for three long months.

I always talked to my family and friends who left Syria on Facebook and WhatsApp and I wanted to tell them what was happening to us — how Yasmin died and my school got bombed. Mummy said that there are more people on Twitter than Facebook, so I could tell people there. She made me an account so we could send messages.

Now I could tell people about how we didn't have any food or medicine and how bad the bombs were. I didn't know if anyone would listen or care, but I hoped that they would please do something to stop the war.

I've always liked to talk to people and make new friends, and on Twitter I could talk to people all over the world. Mummy and I could speak English, so we could speak to people in the UK and America on Twitter. I thought that maybe they

could help us.

We started getting messages right away from grown-ups and kids all over the world. I couldn't believe that people were listening. And they wrote back such kind things. Mummy and I would read the messages when we had to hide in the basement for hours and hours. When I read the messages, it made me feel like people cared about us, that we weren't all alone. That maybe someone would do something before it was too late.

I Was Afraid People Wouldn't Believe Us.

I wanted to write on Twitter every day to tell people how bad it was in Aleppo and to tell them when I was scared, which was a lot. But it was also fun to tell the world about nice things too, like when I lost my teeth.

Mummy would help me figure out what to say in English. We also took many pictures and videos so the world could see what was happening in Syria. I was afraid people wouldn't believe us if they didn't see how bad it was, like all the dead bodies and crumbled buildings.

I tried to tell people every time something bad happened, like what happened to my friend Marwa, who was seven like me. That day, there was a sound like an earthquake, but we didn't hear any planes. We ran to the window and could see a giant cloud of smoke and dust in the air. We ran to the building where the smoke was, and it was terrible. It was an apartment building like my family's, with four families living inside, just like mine. It had collapsed, and all the people inside were in the rubble. The neighbors said twenty people lived there. The volunteers came and dug all day, trying to get all the people out. They found them, but no one was still alive.

We left when the sun went down, and Baba took me with him to the market. We were sad after the long day of digging and death, and Baba was going to try to find something to cheer us up. Maybe there would be a treat, even though there hadn't been any sweets in a long time. At the market, everyone said that Marwa's father and brother had been missing all day. Another man said he heard they were going to help fix a certain building that morning. It was the same building that had collapsed. Baba called some neighbors, and we all came back and started searching again.

There was so much rubble; because it was an entire building, we couldn't dig with just our hands, so we had a bulldozer too. Marwa and her mummy were crying a lot. I hugged her and told her we would find them. We all hurried to dig as fast as we could. Marwa and I couldn't lift the big rocks, but we helped with the little ones. We dug for hours; Mummy let me stay and help. But we didn't find anything. Mummy said I had to go to bed, but I could come back tomorrow to help. So I did. And I went back the next day too. Every day, I kept telling Marwa that we should have hope. She said she didn't want to be without her baba. She already missed him. But they might not be in the rubble after all. Or maybe even if they were, they would be okay.

But they weren't okay. After a week we found them — it was too late. When a body is dead from bombing, it looks crumpled up like a building, and gray like a building too. And the body is floppy, and sometimes parts come off like a leg or an arm, or even a face. It is not something you ever want to see.

I thought maybe if people around the world saw how bad it was and knew how many people were dying — like a whole family and Marwa's baba and brother in one minute — they would help us.

#StandwithAleppo

I was excited when I could see the number of people following my Twitter feed grow and grow — it was fun to count them. I was sure that all these people all over the world could help us stop the war.

Mummy and I decided to make a hashtag so that we could spread the word about Aleppo and get people to support us and maybe save us. I put #StandwithAleppo in my post, and around the world everyone used the hashtag too, more than one million times.

People were starting to learn more and care more about how bad it was in Syria, and I helped with that! I just didn't want people to forget about us, and I wanted them to keep sending me nice messages about how much they cared about me. Every time I got one, it made us feel better.

I was making so many friends all over the world. And some people from the news wanted to talk to me. A journalist named Ahmad Hasan who also lived in Aleppo came to our house to meet me. I wore my favorite skirt and a nice white shirt for our meeting. I was a little nervous because I had never been interviewed by a reporter before. He was very nice, though. I showed him how I could read and write in English, and he said I was very clever. He asked me why I went on Twitter, and I told him that I was tired of the war and sad that my school was bombed and my friends were killed. I wanted people to help us. He told me he thought I was helping people, and that made me feel good.

Other people from Aleppo said I was helping too. When they saw me on the street, if I was taking videos or pictures, they would say "Thank you, Bana" and "Good for you, Bana," and sometimes they tweeted to me. We all thought the world had forgotten us, so they liked that I was telling people not to forget East Aleppo.

The people who helped to fix the Wi-Fi always came to our neighborhood to check to make sure the Wi-Fi and the cables worked after a bombing. They said it was important for me to be able to keep telling the world what was happening.

Even if we all got bombed away, someone

would know what happened to us. We could at least say good-bye.

"You Will Face Death."

The planes came, and instead of dropping bombs, they dropped pieces of paper. The papers said: *This area will be destroyed, and you will face death. You must leave at once.* The government also sent texts to warn us that in twenty-four hours terrible bombing would start.

The regime decided they were going to bomb East Aleppo street by street so that anybody in the Free Syrian Army who was in East Aleppo would be killed. But we were there too.

They said we must leave, but we had nowhere to go since the army was all around the city. And they could be playing another mean trick and shooting or arresting people who tried to get to West Aleppo. One time earlier in the siege they had dropped papers from the planes all over East Aleppo. They said the government would stop fighting and bombing so that people could cross

الإنذار الأخير

شدة الضربات تتصاعد... القادم أعظم

غداً في تمام الساعة ١٢٫٠٠

سيتم توجيه ضربات ساحقة لهذه المنطقة

over to West Aleppo and be safe. But when some people tried to do that, soldiers shot them, or if men went to West Aleppo, the regime made them fight in their army even if they didn't want to be soldiers. So saying you could go to West Aleppo and be safe was a mean trick.

After the leaflets came, it was very bad. It's hard to think about how bad it was from then on. It was the worst time of our lives.

It used to be that a good day was two bombs and a bad day was ten bombs. Now there were bombs all day and all night with no break, like maybe one hundred bombs, but you couldn't even count them. You can't imagine how bad it is to be where bombs are falling around you, all the time. And these bombs are a different kind — they are even bigger. And there were more chlorine bombs too.

We didn't even sleep anymore because there were too many bombs. And we didn't really even make rice or macaroni that much, because there was never time before the warplanes came again.

At first my brothers and cousins and I all cried when these bombs came, but after a while we stopped — even Noor — because we didn't have any more tears.

Grandma Alabed came over one morning and talked in a serious voice to Mummy and Baba. I wasn't supposed to know, but I overheard her say the army was close and that "our neighborhood was next."

Right away Baba went to get Uncle Wesam and said they would be back later. I didn't want them to go look for the army.

Mummy tried to cheer Grandma up by making her some tea, but I don't think it really helped.

Baba came back later that afternoon before dinner. I was in the living room writing in my journal, and he didn't even come over to give me a hug like he always did when he got back. He went straight to talk to Mummy and Grandma in the kitchen,

with more serious voices.
I could tell it was bad.

LIKE I WAS DEAD,
BUT I WASN'T YET.

It was worse than bad, though; it became the most awful ever.

Baba and the uncles and Grandma were talking in the living room, trying to make a plan for how to get away from the army. Mummy was in the kitchen with Aunt Fatemah making dinner (more rice). I was in the living room still writing in my journal, when suddenly there was the loudest noise, like many sounds all at once: glass breaking, walls falling down, and a crash like something had hit the whole earth.

Then it was like someone punched me very hard and knocked me over. Everything went dark and quiet, like I was dead, but I wasn't yet.

Then so many screams: Mummy, Mohamed, Aunt Fatemah, Lana, everyone yelling and crying at once. I could hear the screams, but I couldn't see anyone. Everything was dark with smoke. There was no air to breathe. I couldn't stop coughing. I couldn't see anything. I was confused, until I realized it had finally happened: a bomb had hit our apartment directly. Everything in it was blown up.

I felt someone's arms around me, and then we were running down the stairs.

We got to the basement, and I saw that it was Uncle Wesam carrying me. He put me down, and I looked around — my aunts and uncles and cousins had run down to the basement too. But no Mummy. Or Baba. I started screaming for them. No one answered me. I was out of breath like I had been running, even though I hadn't been.

Then a minute later Mummy was there, holding Mohamed, covered in dust; she looked like a ghost. She hugged me at the same time she was screaming "Where's Noor? Where's Ghassan?" over and over.

I was so relieved that Mummy was alive that I felt weak. It was like being in a dream and a nightmare at the same time.

All the grown-ups were panicked, especially Grandma Alabed, who was crying the loudest. She was worried about Grandpa, who was at their house. And also about Baba. No one knew what to do.

Someone said the basement wasn't safe. But there was nowhere else to go.

We could hear the bombs coming down around us.

Mummy put Mohamed down, and he crawled over and sat in my lap. She was talking to Uncle Wesam and trying to figure out where Baba was.

"Did you see him? Did you see him? Is he dead?" Mummy kept yelling, and her voice was very high. "Did he get Noor?"

Uncle Wesam told her that he was sure Baba and Noor were fine; that they must have run down the stairs to the other part of the basement.

Mummy was going to go upstairs and back down the other stairs to make sure, but we begged her not to leave. It wasn't safe.

She fell to the ground and kept crying. Every time I thought about how Noor and Baba weren't with us and that they might be dead, I felt very tired, like I just wanted to lie on the ground and go to sleep because it was too hard to be awake.

It was hard to even think at all, though, because the bombs never stopped falling on us, and the walls of the basement were shaking and crumbling.

Mummy rushed over to cover my mouth and Mohamed's with pieces of a ripped shirt so we wouldn't breathe the dust. She put her body on top of ours to protect us from the rocks and parts of the wall that were falling down. We kept getting hit anyway. It was like someone was poking me with something sharp all over. We were all bleeding from different cuts.

Suddenly, Uncle Nezar fell over, and we thought he had died. Mummy said he just passed out. We poured water on him to wake him up.

Then a big piece of wall hit Uncle Mazen. He screamed out, and blood started running from his leg. "I'm okay, I'm okay," he said, but I could tell it hurt very much.

After a while we were all quiet, because there was nothing we could do but sit there and be stoned by the sky.

Our Home Was Gone.

It was many hours before the bombs stopped. I was actually scared for them to stop, because once they did we could go upstairs, and then we would know once and for all if Baba and Noor were dead. I didn't want to find out.

When it got quiet, Uncle Wesam told us to wait and he would go see what was what. He came back with the best news! Baba and Noor were alive. They were in the other basement after all. Mummy couldn't stop crying even though it was good news.

All of us, including Baba and Noor, went up to the street, and we all wanted to take time to hug each other and be happy that we were alive, but there wasn't any time because we knew the planes would be coming back, and we had to find someplace to go.

We waited on the street while Mummy quickly ran up to see if she could get our valuable things, like money. Mummy had grabbed her phone and her purse with some important things that she always kept nearby before she ran to the basement, but she wanted to get Baba's phone and the chargers. I wanted her to get my dolls too. But I looked up, and even in the dark I could tell our house was all smashed up. I knew my books and toys were probably all gone. I felt something that was worse than sadness seeing that our home was destroyed. It was like I was completely black inside.

Suddenly Grandpa Alabed came running up — he was so worried about Grandma. Everyone hugged and cried again. But we still needed to have someplace to go. It was the middle of the night, and it was dangerous to be on the street. Baba and Uncle Wesam decided we should go to Grandpa and Grandma Alabed's building for now — Grandpa said it wasn't hit very bad.

We had to run very fast so that we wouldn't get hit by a bomb. It was pitch-black outside, and that was scary. We could barely see where we were going. Mummy said we couldn't look at or use our phones for light because the planes would see us. Also, it was freezing cold, and we had no shoes. My feet were getting cut up as we ran over all the rubble and shells on the streets. But I had to be a big girl and run, because Baba was carrying Mohamed and Mummy was carrying Noor.

We finally made it to Grandma's building, and we went straight to the basement. It was so cold. Uncle Nezar was the coldest, because his shirt was frozen from the water we had poured on him. So we all huddled together to keep warm. It's nice to have a big family when you need to keep warm.

Even though the sun was coming up now, we were very tired. Mummy snuggled with us until we fell asleep. Usually it was hard to sleep, so we slept only a little here and there when it was quiet, which it almost never was because the planes were always in the sky. But that night I felt more tired than I ever have. I could have slept forever.

It was hard to wake up, because I remembered what had happened: our home was gone. When I woke up, Mummy and Baba were both gone, and that made my heart beat very fast. Grandma Alabed told me to be calm — they just went to see if they could get anything from our house. I hoped they could get my dolls, but I was afraid they were all dead. Even Yasmin.

WHAT WOULD HAPPEN IF THE ARMY FOUND US?

We didn't have a home anymore. I had never not had a home, so I didn't know what was going to happen. Where would we go now? The regime's army was blowing up East Aleppo street by street, day by day, so we had to move farther and farther east, away from the army that was chasing us.

Baba and Uncle Wesam hurried to try to find us a place to go. Baba's friend Abdulrahman said that he knew a place we could stay, but it was too far to walk there. Baba and Uncle Wesam went to try to find us a car. They had to hurry, because the army was coming.

Mummy gathered as much as she could of our belongings, but most of it was all blown up. She showed me the video she took, and I wanted to put it on Twitter so everyone would know that I'd lost my home. The black feeling came back when I looked at the video. Especially when I saw

170

my room.

After Baba had been gone for a while, I started to get worried that the army would find us, or that maybe they had already found him. I wasn't sure what would happen if the army found us. Would they shoot us? Put us in jail? Could we be in jail together? Sometimes I liked to ask Mummy questions, but I was too scared to ask these questions.

Baba and Uncle Wesam came back and ran down to the basement, where we were still waiting. "Let's go, let's go. Hurry!" they said, and we all ran up to the street. I looked at the car they had found; it was a truck with an open back. "Get in!" Baba was hurrying us.

We looked worried because we couldn't all fit. But we had to. So all of us — nineteen people — got into the car. I don't know how we did that. We had to hold on very tightly, because the truck bounced around over the rubble and Baba was driving very fast. I thought we would fall out. Noor was screaming the whole time. I closed my eyes tight so I wouldn't be as scared. It didn't really help, though.

I Had Never Felt
Worse Inside Before.

The new house was so dirty. I hated it as soon as we got in the door. No one had lived in it for a long time, and there was no furniture or food or heat. It wasn't like a real home at all.

Baba and Uncle Wesam left again as soon as we got to the new place. They went to find water. I hoped they would be back soon, because I was so thirsty.

I tried to remember how long it had been since I had had food or water. It gives you an awful feeling in your throat when it's so dry you can barely swallow and in your tummy when it's so empty that it hurts.

I wished I could take a bath. We were so dirty from the dust and the cuts, but we had no way to clean up. And we had no clean clothes to put on anyway. Baba had found us some shoes to wear at a market — they were more like slippers than shoes, but they didn't have any real shoes, and we

172

needed something.

I had never felt worse inside before: hungry and thirsty and tired and scared and sad and freezing cold, since we had no heat or blankets. My ears were still ringing from the bombs too. It was so many bad feelings at the same time that I didn't know what to do. I just lay in Mummy's lap and tried not to think about anything at all.

It Might Have Been That My Heart Was Sick.

I didn't know how long we would stay in this house or whether it was our new home. The only good thing about it was that there weren't many bombs. We had gone far enough away from where the army was that they weren't bombing here as much — just one or two every day.

But that was the only good thing, because everything else was awful. Baba had to try to find water every day, and there was barely any. Since there wasn't any more fuel, it was hard to work the generators, and without the generators people couldn't pump water. So we could drink only one tiny cup a day. We also had only one meal a day. Mummy had found a little bit of flour in our bombed house, and she brought it with her and she made bread, or something like bread, in a pan over a fire. Since there was no fuel, we cooked what food we could find over a fire.

Some neighbors shared a few blankets

with us, but we still slept every night on the cold, dirty floor of this house. I let Noor lay his head on my stomach, since we didn't have any pillows.

I got very sick. It might have been that my heart was sick, and it made my body sick. But all I could do was lie down because I felt so tired. There was no medicine to help me feel better.

I was too tired to have hope anymore. I was tired of fighting to stay alive. I thought it might be easier if a bomb came down on

us and we didn't have to live like this anymore.

We Had Nowhere to Go.

"Get up, get up!" Mummy and Baba were yelling for everyone to wake up, and I didn't know why, because the sun was barely up. We had been living in the empty house for a couple of weeks, and I thought it was our new home. But Mummy said, "Bana, we have to leave now!"

I was so tired and confused.

The neighbors had come in the middle of the night and said that the government army was getting close to us again, so we had to leave now. But just like before, we had nowhere to go.

Everyone was in a panic. Baba had a car outside — it was his friend Abdulrahman's. Baba told all the women and children to get into the car. We barely fit, but he drove away really, really fast. Everyone was pressed against one another.

"Where are we going?" I asked. But no one had any answers. Baba just pulled over and said that we should wait here while he went back to get my uncles.

I had never been to this part of Aleppo before. We didn't know where to go. I held on to Mummy's hand so tight.

We walked around a little, because there was nothing to do. Then we ran into someone we knew! It was Ahmad Hasan, the journalist who had come to interview me about being on Twitter. He was very nice and always wanted to help us. Sometimes, since we didn't have a house anymore, Mummy and I had walked to his office to charge Mummy's phone, or he let us use the Wi-Fi so I could use Twitter.

We told Ahmad that we had no place to go. He said he would help us. He was the only person in his apartment, which was nearby, so our family could go and stay there, and he would go stay at a friend's house.

"Thank you, thank you," Mummy said, and I hugged him. I was so thankful that we would have a place to go. Now we just needed Baba and the uncles to come back so we could tell them.

GOD IS THE BEST PROTECTOR.

The first thing I saw when Baba came back was the blood. He was trying to smile and pretend he was all right, but we all noticed. Mummy ran over as soon as he got out of the car. The car was different than when it dropped us off too — all the doors were banged up and the glass in the front was broken.

"Ghassan! What happened? Are you okay?" Mummy was touching him all over to try to figure out where he was hurt. Uncle Wesam was bleeding too, and Aunt Fatemah was doing the same as Mummy — trying to make him better.

Baba told us that a bomb blew up in front of the car when he went back to get the men. They got hit with shells, just like what happened to Uncle Nezar. Baba didn't get hit in the face, though — just the arm. Uncle Wesam got hit in the back.

We went to Ahmad's house and looked at

the cuts to see if they would be okay. We didn't even have any water to wash them out. Baba kept saying, "I'm fine, I'm fine." But he wasn't fine. I could tell, and that made me very scared. I cried so much — I couldn't help it.

Then I got Mummy's Quran out of her purse. She had gotten it when she did her Hajj, and she kept it in the bag that she had grabbed before our house was bombed, so it was safe.

I always love to read the Quran to Baba (and to my dolls too). I read Baba's favorite verses to him to make us both feel better: *Only God is the best Protector. His mercy is far greater than that of others.*

WE HAD NOWHERE TO RUN.

Our new house had only two rooms and two beds, even though we were nineteen people. We put the mattresses on the floor so we could have a little more room for all the girls to sleep on one and the boys on the other.

Every day we had to figure out how to get the basic things, like food to eat and clean water to drink.

I didn't like to go outside very much. There were so many people on the streets — thousands and thousands of people who, like us, had nowhere to go. Some were just lying on the ground, or they were bleeding, or they were burning things to keep warm.

At the apartment, we were many people packed into a small space, and even when we were outside, it still felt like we were too many people packed into a small space. I didn't like it.

The building we were staying in was all

the way at the end of Aleppo. We had all been pushed there by the army and the bombs. Now there was no place to go. There was nothing else between us and the army tanks. And now they were bombing us a lot and coming toward us with their big guns.

We had nowhere to run.

This was it.

Mummy and I tried to get our friends on Twitter to help us. Maybe they could stop the planes from coming back with bombs.

If they didn't, it would be the end for us.

Bana Alabed ✓
@AlabedBana

Please save us now. - Bana #Aleppo

16 Dec 2016

You Can't Imagine How Happy We Were to Hear This.

Mummy heard back from someone to help us! The foreign minister of Turkey was talking to the regime and people in Iran and Russia and other places so that they would make a cease-fire, which means they would stop the fighting and bombing so that we would be able to leave Aleppo.

There were going to be buses that would come pick up everyone who was trapped and drive them away from Aleppo to somewhere where they would be safe. On the first day the buses would pick up the injured people and the very sick people, and then on the days after that the buses would come back and pick up all the other people who wanted to leave.

You can't imagine how happy we were to hear this. I thought I would be sad to think about leaving Aleppo, but I wanted to have food and water and a place to sleep more than anything else — even if that wasn't in

Aleppo anymore.

The next day Mummy and I went to someone she knew who was working at a hospital nearby. She asked if she could please help us get out on the first buses with the sick people, since my baba was still hurt. But Mummy's friend said there was nothing she could do.

I don't like to think about what I saw outside the hospital: hundreds of people lying all over the ground who were hurt and bleeding. Many were crying and moaning. And a lot of people who had their eyes closed, who I hoped were just sleeping. The air smelled very bad — worse than when the tires were burning. It is a smell I will never forget, no matter how much I want to.

I Had to Get
to Those Buses.

Baba didn't think we should go on the first day of the buses — he wanted to wait and see what would happen and if it would be safe. Grandma Alabed still wanted to try; she thought we might have only one chance. I wanted to leave too — I wanted to be anywhere except where we were. But Baba is clever and a good leader of our family and knows what is best. That night we heard that a lot of people had been able to leave. That was good news and made us excited to go the next day.

We left early in the morning, before the sun, to try to be in the front of the line for the buses. It was so crowded already, though, that we couldn't even see the front of the line or the buses themselves. People had been sleeping on the street, waiting, so there were a lot of people ahead of us. All we could do was wait too. But we didn't have any food or water, and it was freezing

cold, the kind of cold that makes you shiver all over. We made a fire to keep warm, but I still couldn't feel my nose, toes, or fingers.

In the afternoon we heard screaming and loud pops. They were shooting at people who were trying to get on the buses. All the people waiting were upset and panicked — especially Grandma. She yelled, "I knew we should have left yesterday! We will never get out now!" All of us tried to get her to calm down, but it was okay to be upset, because this was a very bad thing. What if there were no more buses now?

We went back to the apartment, and Mummy and I went on Twitter and told everyone that the cease-fire was broken. There was nothing we could do, but maybe our friends in other places could get the soldiers to keep their promise not to hurt the people who were just trying to escape.

The next day, we heard more bad news: now there were no buses. It was a very bad day, because we had no hope. All we could do was pray that the buses would come back.

The day after that we got up again before the sun and went to where the buses were and prayed no one would shoot us. This time there were fewer people — maybe because they were scared. I could see the buses! They were there! They were big, and there were many of them to make a long chain like a snake.

It was the best sight ever. I started crying. I was crying because I was so happy — that had never happened to me before. I thought you cried only when you were sad.

I grabbed Mummy's hand and started to run toward them. I had to get to those

buses. Noor and Mohamed started screaming and running too. "The buses, the buses!"
They were yelling and kind of laughing,
kind of crying.

"Wait, wait, let's see if it's safe!" Mummy
was trying to hold me back.

But I didn't want to go back. I wanted to
get on a bus that day so we wouldn't have
to go back to the apartment. I never wanted
to go back there. I begged Mummy and
Baba to run, so we all did. We got separated
from some other parts of our family in the
crowds, but we could tell there would be
room for everyone.

We got on the bus. Finally.

I Almost Couldn't Even Believe It.

We were so excited to leave and get to a safe place, away from the bombs. But the buses didn't move. I couldn't understand why. We waited and waited, and they didn't go anywhere. First it was one hour, and then two, and then many, many hours. The sun went down, and we still didn't move. No one could get on or off the bus. We were trapped. We had no food or water. It was so cold that we could see the air come out of our mouths. And that wasn't even the worst part: the worst part was that no one had a way to go to the bathroom. So everyone was going to the bathroom in their pants — especially the kids — so the bus had the worst smell you could possibly imagine.

It was so dark in the night when we were sitting on the bus — no light at all, and nothing to do but wait. We felt like a bomb was going to fall on us or that soldiers were going to come in. Nobody said anything, because everyone was too sad and scared. It was so quiet — except for all the babies who were crying because they were so hungry and had dirty nappies. We were like prisoners, and the bus was our jail. What if we had to stay on the bus forever?

Mummy had some mobile service, so she sent a quick message to the Turkish government to see if they could help us.

The sun came up the next day, and we were all still awake. All of a sudden, we heard the loud sound of engines, and the buses started moving. We thought it was a dream. We drove for twenty minutes, and then out the window we could see a big crowd of people who were waiting for us. Mummy said they were people who were going to help us. I could see myself in the window, and I had the biggest smile on my face that maybe I have ever had. It made my cheeks hurt. I almost couldn't even believe it — we were safe.

WE ARE SAFE NOW.

My legs felt shaky when I got off the bus, like I had forgotten how to stand after sitting for so long. There were nice people there who had so much food and so much water to give to us and to all the people from the other buses. We learned that there was a woman from another bus who had even had a baby, and there were doctors who came to help her.

Mohamed said, "Mummy! We are in heaven!" And that is how we all felt. We hadn't eaten in so long that we didn't know what to eat first. We wanted everything at the same time — bananas and apples and bread! And water. The water tasted so good. I had three bottles in a row. But then we all threw up from eating and drinking so much. So we took a break and then ate again.

After I ate and cleaned up, there was a man there who asked me and Mummy to talk on TV and tell everyone about Aleppo

and how it felt to be safe.

After that, a doctor invited my family to his house nearby to clean up. When we got there, some men who worked with the Turkish government came to get us so we would be safe. The Syrian government didn't like it that I was on Twitter and wanted peace, so it wasn't good for us to stay where we were, which was still in Syria but in the countryside.

First we had to drive in a car to another

town near the border, and then we flew on a plane to Turkey. I had never been in the sky before. My stomach had a weird feeling when the plane went into the air. It was partly that I was scared to fly, and also that I was a little afraid and sad to leave Syria. In the plane, I looked down to see if I could see Aleppo and wave good-bye. But it was dark out, and I could only see some lights. The world looks so pretty from up in the air — all the tiny buildings and lights, like a dollhouse. I couldn't imagine how you could drop bombs on it.

We were all quiet looking out the window. Baba leaned back and closed his eyes. Noor and Mohamed had fallen asleep. Mummy was sitting across the aisle from me. She leaned over and whispered, "We are safe now, Bana. We are going to be okay."

That was the last thing I remember before I fell asleep too. I dreamed I was swimming with Baba, and he and I were splashing each other with water. I was laughing and laughing; I was so happy.

The future is uncertain, Bana. But we know that we have survived the worst days of our lives. There is some comfort in that, knowing that we will never again have to endure the terror and the chaos and the deprivations we did in our last few weeks and months in Syria — at least, outside of our nightmares.

The suffering, the death, the fear, the thirst and hunger, day in and day out, with no end in sight — it took its toll on all of us. I could see the effects of malnutrition and stress in you children: the dark circles under your eyes, your thinning hair, your scared silences. The fear when I had no medicine to give you when you had an asthma attack and when you got very ill. We survived a hell on earth that few people can imagine or comprehend.

It is hard for me to say this. But for all my wanting to always be strong for you, to not show my fear, to make our lives as happy as possible under the brutal circumstances, there came a moment when I didn't think I could go on. Our home had been destroyed, which was devastating, and for weeks we were refugees in our own city. I had seen you children suffering and witnessing horrific sights no child should — dead bodies rotting in the streets — knowing there was little I could do to shield you or make things better. Then neighbors came and told us the regime was advancing. We had been pushed and pushed to the farthest corner of the city like mice in a maze. Now, quite literally, we had nowhere to go. We were completely surrounded in back and in front and in the air above by the advancing army.

Baba and I sat huddled together in the freezing cold outside, in the pitch-black night. The only light came from a few distant fires. The smell of burning nylon and wood came on the wind, and the stink of oil and rotting flesh, which always hung in the air. We allowed our worst thoughts and fears to overtake us, and there was an odd comfort in that. After all we had endured, it had come to this. "It is over." I think I said that out loud, and instead of fear, I felt something like relief. I was exhausted from the sheer effort it took to survive. After fighting to live for so long, I considered that it might be nice to let go, to let the current drag me under — to leave this world for the next.

Perhaps death was the only way to have peace.

But the will to live is strong — like your breath or your heartbeat, it carries you even if you're not conscious of it. It is a flame that flickers deep within. This is why so many of us are able to carry on, even when it is easier to die or to give up. We have so much capacity for suffering; it is shocking what we can bear. We take what comes and we endure. We find a way to go forward.

And so it was that even in that, my darkest hour, I could summon reasons to live — mainly you children. And also so that I could help others. You and I had become a voice for the people of Syria, and we couldn't let the people down.

It is a strange thing, but in many ways, Twitter saved us, Bana. Literally and figuratively. It gave us a way to connect to people who could help us, who were able to keep you safe and allow us to escape Aleppo. But also because connecting with other people and sharing our story made us feel better. It gave us purpose and strength — it still does. Our world in the basement was tiny, but with a simple mobile phone it became vast.

The children in Syria had no way to speak for themselves, so you spoke for them. From the time you were little, you were outraged by injustices. You would say "That is not right" or "That is not fair" whenever you saw something that didn't agree with your strong moral code. And during the war, you were convinced that if people understood what was happening, they would help us. And they did. We are safe, but we still have more work to do to end the war once and for all.

We will not be silent until that happens. Even when they try to discredit you or bully you or, worst of all, silence you. Is there a more shameful act than to threaten the life of a seven-year-old girl? My blood ran cold the day I got the first death threats toward you, from awful Twitter trolls and the regime. And also when we learned that the regime bombed our house on purpose, that we were a particular target. I felt sick to my stomach.

I worried for your life those last few weeks especially. I felt like we were being hunted, and the rest of the family was very concerned that you were at special risk, and so we all were at special risk. I took out the SIM card on my phone so that the regime couldn't track us, and I made sure you always wore your hat when we went out of the house. I didn't want anyone from the army to recognize you. It helped that you were wearing boys' clothes along with your hair being hidden. I remember how much you cried when you got those clothes — but they turned out to be a saving grace.

I would and will do anything to keep you safe, Bana, but I will not silence you. That is what they want. That is what they've tried to do to peacemakers since the beginning of time: Jesus, Martin Luther King Jr., Gandhi.

But that just speaks to how powerful your message is. You can change the world, and they know that. So we will not back down to the bullies and cowards who want to hurt a little girl when all she wants is peace.

We must continue to speak out on behalf of innocent Syrians and other people affected by war. We understand what is at stake and just how hideous war is, so if not us, then who? We lived, and our debt and our duty for that miracle is to help others to live.

And what does the future hold for us? We don't know. All you and your brothers have known is a life of war and violence, and it will take time for those scars to heal — but already you are laughing more, and there is a lightness I haven't seen before in you and Mohamed and Noor. And Noor said his first words a week after we arrived in Turkey, and now he is a little chatterbox. Baba and I joke that we miss when he didn't talk. What a gift to be able to joke.

I have modest dreams for the future, Bana.

I want for us to create a new home for our family and to fill it with things that we love. I want you and your brothers to get a good education. I want to be able to finish university, and your baba would like to find work to support us, maybe open up a shop. We want what everybody wants, what everybody has always wanted since the beginning of time: a simple and happy life.

There is something clarifying about survival, and that comes from losing everything — your country, your home, your belongings. When stripped of everything, you understand what you are made of and what is essential.

You are essential, and Baba, and Noor and Mohamed and the rest of our family. We are all we need.

We will always miss Syria. Every day you still ask when we can go home. I hope that day will come, that we will see a country that is rebuilt and a people reborn. That may be a long time from now, though. Maybe you will have given me grandchildren by then. I will tell them stories about the war and how brave their mother was, how you never gave up and how you made it your mission to help people. How you spread a message of hope and peace.

I will tell them that their mother is a hero.

You are, Bana. And I am so proud to be your mother.

I love you, Bon Bon, more than you can ever know.

Love,
Mummy

THIS IS MY WISH.

Did you know that the war in Syria has killed about five hundred thousand people, and many more are still getting hurt and dying every day? Many families like mine had no choice but to leave the country we love to go to other places where we are refugees. Some people say that they don't want refugees in their country. They want them to go home, even though they have no home anymore. Or to go somewhere else, even though the people "somewhere else" might not welcome them either. But there is no place else for people to go. If you had no country or your parents or children were going to be killed, what would you do?

When you go to someone's house in Syria, we welcome you as if you are family and share whatever we have, like tea or sweets. That is how I wish it could be if someone comes to your country — that you share with them and help them and try to understand what they have been through.

People in Turkey have been nice to my family, and I am grateful for that. We are lucky, because some refugees from Syria and other places have to live in camps. Some camps are crowded, and there is not enough food or medicine and people have nothing to do all day, like work or school.

I went to visit a camp in Reyhanlı, Turkey, and they are trying to make a nice place for people to live, but it's still not the same as having a home. I went to visit an orphanage in Gaziantep, Turkey, and there were more than twenty-five children there whose parents had died in the war. I am so lucky that I still get to have both of my parents. But many children don't get to have them. And children are still dying and getting hurt every day — like Abdulbaset Ta'an, a little boy I visited in the hospital who is almost the same age as me and lost his legs to a bomb.

It is not right that people have to live in camps, or live in fear all the time, or see their friends and family die, or live without clean water or food or a home. And when you know something is not right, you have to fix it. We all have to help one another, no matter what country we live in.

I am helping people by bringing attention

to war and how bad it is — especially for children.

You can help too. You could help by giving money to people who are helping Syrians, like organizations that are working to help the plight of refugees.

Or you could talk to other people in your country and write letters to your presidents, prime ministers, and politicians and ask them to help.

Or you could be nice to a refugee family and see if they need help learning about their new country. Remember, they are homesick.

You could also pray or make a wish, like when you blow out birthday candles or throw a penny into a fountain.

I turned eight while I was working on my

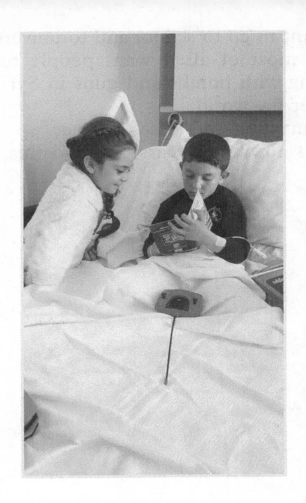

book, so I got to make a wish when I was blowing out my candles.

It was hard to decide on only one wish, because I have many, like:

I want to never have to hear or see a bomb again.

I want to be able to go home to live in Aleppo one day.

I want a baby sister.

I want to go to school and to university.

But most of all, I want people to stop fighting with bombs and guns in Syria and all over the world.

I want there to please be peace.

I am now eight years old, and this is my wish.

I would like to thank everybody who helped to publish this book. It would not have been possible without my family and many friends. Christine PRIDE my editor, was very supportive and encouraging. I would also like to thank my agent Zoe King who walked the walk with me every step of the way to publishing day. And finally, I would like to thank J.K Rowling for being an inspiring energy to me.
Thank you all.

Bana

ABOUT THE AUTHOR

Bana Alabed, born in 2009 in Aleppo, Syria, is known worldwide for her tweets during the siege of the city in 2016 and for her subsequent calls for peace and an end to all global conflict. Her tweets have earned her legions of admirers around the world by giving a remarkable insight into the daily horrors of life in the city, including airstrikes, hunger, and the prospect of her family's death. In December 2016, Bana and her family were safely evacuated from Aleppo to Turkey. When she grows up, Bana would like to become a teacher, like her mother. Her father is a lawyer, and she has two younger brothers, Noor and Mohamed. *Dear World* is her first book.

The employees of Thorndike Press hope you have enjoyed this Large Print book. All our Thorndike, Wheeler, and Kennebec Large Print titles are designed for easy reading, and all our books are made to last. Other Thorndike Press Large Print books are available at your library, through selected bookstores, or directly from us.

For information about titles, please call:
(800) 223-1244

or visit our website at:
gale.com/thorndike

To share your comments, please write:
Publisher
Thorndike Press
10 Water St., Suite 310
Waterville, ME 04901